Dedication

This book is dedicated to Marland Williams, who faced life's
challenges head-on.
To his papa, he was Kid.
His soldier buddies nicknamed him Bill.
In Cannon Falls, people knew him as Doc Williams.
To me, he was Grampa.

— Elizabeth Williams Gomoll

D1310316

ENLISTMENT RECORD.

Name: *Marland R Williams*   Grade: *Mus 3d Class*

Enlisted *Apr 20*, 1917, at *Duluth Minn*

*In the service of the United States, under call of the President, from _____ to _____

Serving in *First* _____ enlistment period at date of discharge.

Prior service: † *None*

_____

Noncommissioned officer: *None*

Marksmanship, gunner qualification or rating: ‡ *None*

Horsemanship: *None*

Battles, engagements, skirmishes, expeditions: *None*

_____

Knowledge of any vocation: *Student*

Wounds received in service: *None*

Physical condition when discharged: *Good*

Typhoid prophylaxis completed *Not completed*

Paratyphoid prophylaxis completed *Not completed*

Married or single: *Single*

Character: *Excellent*

Remarks: _____

_____

Signature of soldier: *Marland R. Williams*

Walter O Floding
Capt 3d Minn Inf N.G.
Commanding *Hqtrs Co*

* Strike out line if the soldier was not in the Federal service during this enlistment.
† Give company and regiment or corps or department, with inclusive dates of service in each enlistment.
‡ Give date of qualification or rating and number, date, and source of order announcing same.

3—3966

Table of Contents

Artifacts of War 1

Fully American 2

Coming Late to the Great War 6

Transcribing the Letters 8

Letters from Marland 10

Letters from Stanley 92

Photographs 131

Scrapbook 137

Life After the War 144

Sources 147

Index 149

Artifacts of War

As a genealogist, my home has become a repository for family documents, photographs, certificates, and all manner of three-dimensional heirlooms. Space concerns aside, I am truly honored to be the keeper of these tangible links to my family's ancestors.

A significant part of this collection relates to the World War I military service of Marland and Stanley Williams. First, I was given a thick stack of their letters from 1917 to 1919. Months later a different relative sent Marland's photo album from his time in the army. Over time, more items found their way to my home: military service documents, Marland's wonderful double-bell euphonium, Stanley's doughboy helmet, Marland's uniform, and more.

Marland Williams was my paternal grandfather; his brother Stanley was my great-uncle. When I grew up, children were to be "seen, not heard" when around elders. As a result, I did not know either my grandfather or Uncle Stan on a deeply personal basis, but still, they were very significant people in my life.

The fact that their parents and sisters lovingly saved these eighty-nine letters written by Marland and Stanley is evidence of how they yearned for their boys to come home safely. Did they anticipate the letters might be meaningful to future generations?

Although Stanley spent more than a year at the front and Marland arrived just before Armistice Day, their letters largely describe the highs and lows of camp life in the U.S. and Europe. They also illustrate how frustratingly slow long-distance communication was a century ago.

Always looking for a way to make a buck, Marland did laundry for other soldiers—ten cents for a shirt, fifteen cents for a pair of trousers—until he had enough money to buy a Kodak camera. Then he took photographs and sold prints to his fellow soldiers to send home to their families and sweethearts. Except where noted, the photographs in this book are from Marland's album. Stanley's section sorely lacks photographs. In his letter dated May 28, 1918, he wrote, "I had a camera of my own, but we are not allowed to use them so it don't do me much good."

Both Marland and Stanley concluded their letters with the same phrase: "With love to all." This seems a fitting title for an amalgamation of correspondence to their dear ones at home from the boy musician and his big brother who answered the call to serve their country in The Great War.

Elizabeth Williams Gomoll
North Oaks, Minnesota
2017

Marland, left, and Stanley Williams

Fully American

Stanley and Marland Williams were the oldest of four children born to Swedish immigrants. Their father, Alvin Peterson, was just a toddler when he came to America in 1869 with his parents and three older siblings. Their mother, Hulda Larson, made the voyage by herself at the age of 18 in 1889. They were married on January 23, 1895, at Svea Lutheran Church in the Town of Trenton, Pierce County, Wisconsin.

The young couple settled on a rented farm a short wagon ride from the church and near most of Alvin's large extended family. Children soon followed. Lawrence Stanley was born December 19, 1895. Marland Reinhold—affectionately known as "Kid"—was born June 5, 1899. Their sister, Olga Serafia Constantine, joined the family on May 22, 1903, and Jewell Hazel Mildred came five years later on May 4, 1908.

When they arrived in the United States, Alvin's family name was Peterson. By 1911 there were so many Petersons in the Svea area—a predominantly Swedish community—that Alvin went to the Pierce County courthouse and formally changed his last name to Williams. His older brother Oscar had made this name change years earlier by "Americanizing" his second name, Wilhelm. He was thereafter known as O. P. Williams. Brother Arvid followed suit. While five younger siblings remained Petersons, the three brothers and their families—and the generations that followed—were known as Williams.

Alvin had something of a "grass-is-greener" disposition. He alternated several times between running a general store and farming. Consequently, the family moved at least six times while the children were young, and they attended whatever one-room schoolhouse was within walking distance of their current home. Perhaps this inconsistent schooling explains Marland's casual spelling and punctuation in the letters he wrote home while in the army. For their secondary education, Marland and Stanley attended Red Wing Seminary in Red Wing on the Minnesota side of the Mississippi River. They boarded at the school during the week and walked the six miles home for the weekends, bringing their dirty laundry with them.

Music was valued in this family. Alvin played the piano, and occasionally the pump organ for church services. All four children learned to play musical instruments. Stanley took up the saxophone. Both girls had piano lessons. Marland started on violin at age ten. At Red Wing Seminary he was given a trumpet to play in the band, but he later switched to the baritone. This may have influenced his assignment to the Third Minnesota Infantry Band.

When Marland refers to a place called Svea in his letters, he may mean the Svea Church, or the community around the church and small general store that sat kitty-corner across a gravel road. In 1912, Alvin seized an opportunity to run that country store and painted the name of the establishment on the front in proud block letters: Alvin Williams General Merchandise. A house was moved from another part of town and attached to the store to provide living quarters for the family.

When the United States entered the Great War, Stanley was quick to respond. On April 23, 1917, just 17 days after war was declared, he joined the Fort Snelling-based Minnesota National Guard's 1st Field Artillery. Just one week after Stanley enlisted, 17-year-old Marland received his parents' blessing to sign up. He traveled by train to Duluth, Minnesota, where he enrolled in the National Guard's Third Minnesota Infantry on April 30, 1917.

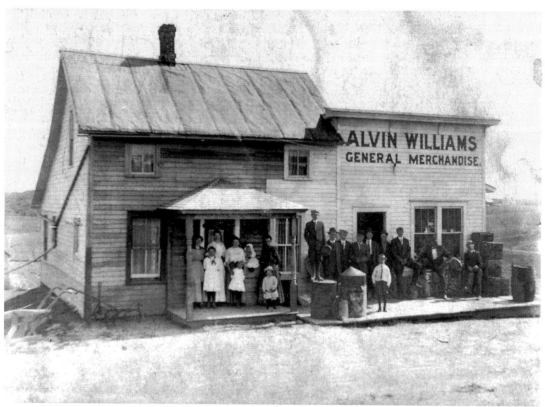

Alvin Williams General Merchandise store and home, ca. 1913. Alvin is sitting in front of the store window, hand on his hip, right foot up on a sack. Stanley stands just to Alvin's right. Marland is standing atop a barrel, holding his violin by the neck. Mother Hulda is on the house porch with Jewell in front of her. Olga is wearing a white dress with a dark neck scarf crisscrossed in front. Source: Private collection of Janice Torseth, Hager City, Wisconsin. [Postcard]

At the time of their enlistments, Stanley worked as a clerk for Merchants National Bank in St. Paul, Minnesota, and Marland attended school in Red Wing. Their departure may have precipitated the family's move to St. Paul in October 1917. There, Alvin was assisted by his wife, Hulda, and daughters, Olga and Jewell, in operating Alvin Williams Grocery Store at 319 Arundel Street. Their living quarters were upstairs.

From these letters, one senses that the members of this family were truly devoted to one another. Marland teased his sister Olga about her weight–though it probably wasn't funny to her. He refers to his brother as "Standley" and signs some of his letters "Kid." Stanley tells his parents to remind Marland that he is their "big boy" and that his little brother will need more pockets to collect souvenirs.

Sadly, about eighty percent of the records for U.S. Army personnel in World War I were destroyed in 1973 when fire broke out at the National Personnel Records Center in St. Louis, Missouri. It is fortunate that so many of Marland and Stanley's letters and other documents have been preserved to tell us about their experience in the Great War.

—E. W. G.

Svea Lutheran Church, located three miles north of Hager City, Wisconsin

Alvin and Hulda Williams, with daughters Olga and Jewell (in front)

Confirmation photo of Marland and Stanley's sister Olga, 1918

National Guard of the United States

AND OF THE STATE OF _Minnesota_

To all whom it may concern:

This is to Certify, That _Marland R Williams_
* _Mus 3d Class Hqts Co Third Minn Inf_
† _National Guard_ as a TESTIMONIAL OF HONEST AND FAITHFUL

SERVICE, is hereby HONORABLY DISCHARGED from the NATIONAL GUARD of the

UNITED STATES and of the State of _Minnesota_ by reason of

‡ _Draft in to U S service_

Said _Marland R Williams_ was born

in _Trenton_, in the State of _Wisconsin_

When enlisted he was _18_ years of age and by occupation a _Student_

He had _Blue_ eyes, _Light_ hair, _Light_ complexion, and

was _5_ feet _9_ inches in height.

Given under my hand at _Duluth Minn_ this

_5th_ day of _Aug_, one thousand nine hundred and _seventeen_

Hubick Berg

Col. 3rd Minn Inf N.G.

Commanding.

Form No. 525-1, A. G. O.
(For National Guard.)
Ed. July 18-17—400,000.

* Insert grade and company and regiment or corps or department; e. g., "Sergeant, Company A, 1st New York Infantry;" "Corporal, Georgia Quartermaster Corps;" "Private, First Class, Illinois Ordnance Department."
† Insert "National Guard" or "National Guard Reserve," as the case may be.
‡ If discharged prior to expiration of service, give number, date, and source of order or description of authority therefor.

3—3966

Coming Late to the Great War

For nearly three years, August 1914 to April 1917, the United States scrupulously avoided entanglement in Europe's disastrous Great War. Multi-million-man armies of the Allied nations—primarily France, Russia, Great Britain and Italy—had faced off against the Central Powers—Germany, Austria-Hungary, the Ottoman Empire and their partners. The combined military death toll now approached a catastrophic four million.

United States President Woodrow Wilson had won re-election in 1916 using the slogan "He kept us out of war." But Germany's January 31, 1917, announcement that its submarines would attack any ships destined for Great Britain had resulted in the sinking of American vessels. Aggressive German political scheming and espionage that targeted America also led Wilson to ask Congress for a declaration of war against Germany. The lawmakers voted for war on April 6, 1917.

America was woefully unprepared to fight. The United States Regular Army totaled a paltry 80,804 officers and men. When troops defending the nation's far-flung territories and manning coastal defenses at home were subtracted, just 24,602 Regular Army soldiers were available for war in spring 1917. The army possessed only a handful of artillery pieces and machine guns, no modern aircraft, and no units of division size. Once fully trained and integrated into the American army, 180,000 national guardsmen would add to that force. Nonetheless, a massive draft of civilians would be needed to meet the three-million soldier goal thought necessary for the Great War, now also becoming known as the "World War."

Orders to mobilize reached the Minnesota National Guard on July 15. On August 27, after being federalized into the U.S. Army, the former guardsmen boarded trains and headed for Camp Cody, New Mexico, to undergo final training. Guardsmen from the Dakotas, Iowa and Nebraska joined them, together forming the U.S. Army's 34th Infantry Division.

The Minnesota National Guard's 1st Field Artillery, meanwhile, had more experience and was ready for rapid deployment. When federalized, that regiment became the 151st Field Artillery, among the first American formations sent to France and combat.

This book is constructed around the letters and photographs of Marland and Stanley Williams, two patriotic brothers who, within three weeks of America's declaration of war, volunteered for military service. Both men would serve in France. Fortunately for history's sake, the brothers enjoyed writing letters home detailing their wartime experiences. Marland's evocative photography amply illustrates the roles these young men played in the Great War of 1914–1918.

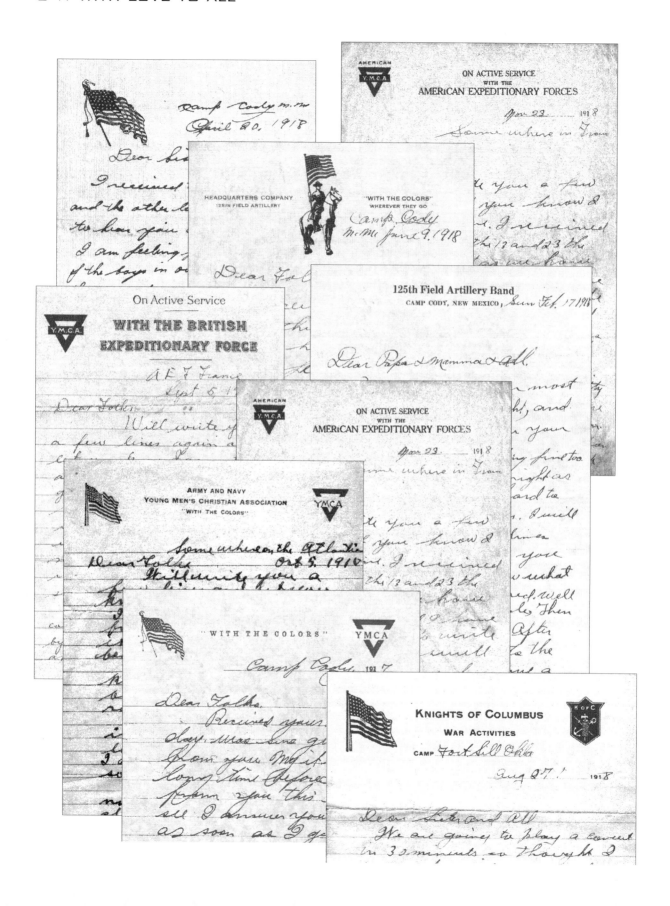

Transcribing the Letters

Marland's letters were scrawled in pencil or pen on whatever writing paper was available. Most of his older brother's letters were neatly typed, as his rank and post gave him access to a typewriter. Marland's newsy letters are full of misspellings, dropped words, and other indications that they were hastily written. Stanley's typed letters have fewer errors, but nonetheless, mistakes do appear.

To maintain their original composition and feel, these letters have been transcribed exactly as written. Spelling, punctuation and choice of words have been retained. Obvious errors have not been noted, as frequent insertions of a bracketed "sic" would disrupt the letters' flow.

Some of the paper upon which Marland and Stanley wrote had organizational logos—Red Cross, YMCA, etc. Such logos have not been replicated on individual letters here, but any letterhead wording has been included. A representation of the original letterheads is found on the adjacent page. Stanley usually typed his own letterhead at the top of his letters. All of the letters of Marland and Stanley Williams included in this book are in the possession of the editor.

Editorial Symbols and Insertions

• Brackets [ ] enclose missing and clarifying words supplied by the editor. They also enclose brief informational comments by the editor or historiographer.

• More lengthy contextual explanations by the editor or historiographer are indicated by a different font and layout.

• Dollar amounts mentioned in 1917 and 1918 letters have been adjusted using the online inflation calculator, www.usinflationcalculator.com. Dollar equivalents for 2016 are shown in brackets.

• Historiographer Frederick L. Johnson provided additional material that places in historical context the wartime experiences of Marland and Stanley Williams and the First World War military operations involving their Minnesota artillery regiments.

Marland R. Williams, Musician 2nd Class
Headquarters Co., 125th Field Artillery, Sandstorm Division

Letters from Marland

Seventeen-year-old Marland Williams joined the Duluth National Guard's Headquarters Company on April 30, 1917, as Musician 3rd Class. After being federalized into the Regular Army, the Guard unit, part of the 34th Minnesota Infantry, was ordered to Camp Cody, New Mexico, for training.[1]

Marland and his buddies dutifully began the change from citizen to soldier. In October, U.S. Army orders reorganized elements of the 34th Infantry into artillery outfits. The 34th adopted the nickname "Sandstorm Division" for the hot, dry desert climate and dust storms around Camp Cody. Musician Williams, a baritone player, became part of the regiment's band. Their training was extended to nearly a year, which frustrated the soldiers—including Marland—who hoped to see combat in France.[2]

During off-duty hours at Camp Cody, Marland busied himself taking photographs. He possessed a wide range of interests that produced around 350 images detailing camp life. The camera seemed to go everywhere Marland went.

On July 2, 1918, after 11 months of training, the 125th Field Artillery boarded an east-bound train for advanced artillery work at Fort Sill, Oklahoma. Nine weeks later, trains took the men to Long Island, New York; they shipped out for Europe on September 24, arriving in England on October 7. The artillerymen reached France on October 10, and a month later headed for the front lines. The war ended before they saw action.

Musician 2nd Class Marland Williams received his discharge from the service at Camp Grant, Illinois, on February 5, 1919.

SPECIAL! ANNOUNCEMENT

The Entertainment Committee of the

Soldiers Carnival

At Eveleth Has Arranged for the Famous

Third Minnesota Band

To appear in a Concert at Virginia in the afternoon and in a Parade and Concert at Eveleth in the evening

FRIDAY August 17

Your opportunity to see the boys of Company F and the Third Minnesota Band in uniform before they leave for their training camp --- and France.

1. Enlistment Record, Marland R. Williams, April 30, 1917, Duluth, Minnesota, a copy is on page 7.

2. Franklin F. Holbrook and Livia Appel, *Minnesota in the War with Germany* (St. Paul: Minnesota Historical Society, 1928), contains a chapter on the training at Camp Cody. For those interested in more detail about the Minnesotans training at Camp Cody, see the *Weekly Bulletin*, a newsletter produced by members of the 34th Division, in the collections of the Minnesota Historical Society. See also Minnesota National Guard, "History of the 34th Infantry Division," www.minnesotanationalguard.org/units/34id/history.php accessed November 19, 2016.

"Drilling Infantry on the Border"
[Deming, N. Mex., Sept. 3, 1917]

Dear Pa + all.
I am fine and dandy. I had another shot or dose in the arm yesterday so its kind of sore. lot of them are in bed from it. We just got throu cleaning up our tent. got your letter day before yesterday.
Kid

Y.M.C.A.
"WITH THE COLORS"

Camp Cody.[3]
[December] 1917

Dear Folks.

Received your letter to day. was sure glad to hear from you. My it seemed a long time before I heard from you this time. You see I answer your letters as soon as I get them, so you see you only get

3. Camp Cody, near Deming, New Mexico, was established in 1917 as a U.S. Army training camp. Originally named Camp Deming, the name soon changed to Camp Cody to honor William F. Cody, better known as Buffalo Bill, plainsman and promoter of a Wild West show, who died that year. More than 30,000 troops passed through Camp Cody during World War I. Robert Hixson Julyan, "The Place Names of New Mexico," http://demingnewmexico.genealogyvillage.com/index. html#life, Camp Cody.

one for every one I get. so please write often.

I am feeling fine. The weather is nice and warm and every thing is about the same so I realy don't know what to write about. I had a long letter from Orion Ulvin yesterday so I heard all about the school.[4] We were down and had joint band rehearsal this after noon. There were over 300 players there so you see its some big band. We are going to play a concert for General Blocksane New Years morning.[5]

I suppose its nice and cold up there. I would just as soon see a little snow my self. It don't seem at all like winter. Well it will soon be a half a year since I left home. It sure don't seem that long. My time goes fast. I suppose you girls have grown a little too. I suppose your some big ladies now that you live in St Paul and go down town and so on.[6] Well practise hard on the piano. I suppose your quiet a player now. I have had a hard time playing this last week because one of my front fillings fell out and the Dentist made it f___tly by drilling in it. I am going to have it filled next week.

You said mamma wondered how I trimed those balls on that pillow so smoth. They are easy to make. Ill show [you] how to make them when I get home. There is eight skans [skeins] of yarn in it so you see there is quiet a bit of stuff in one.

I suppose you like to go to shows. I would like to go my self. I have only taken in one moving picture show down [in] deming since I come here so you see I do not spend any money on them. I suppose it would be different if I were home. I dont believe I told you what I got for Xmas so I will tell you. I [got] a box from a family in Duluth, and in it was a cake, a box of candie, 2 package gum 2 hershis bars, 1 deck card, one jar

Marland with his baritone, 1917

4. At the time of his enlistment, Marland was enrolled in Red Wing Seminary, an academy, junior college, and seminary in Red Wing, Minnesota. His brother, Stanley, had attended there as well. *Red Wing Seminary archive*, St. Olaf College, Northfield, Minnesota.

5. Marland refers to Major General Augustus P. Blocksom.

6. The Williams family moved to 391 Arundel Street in St. Paul, Minnesota, in October 1917.

of peanut butter and a package of eating raisins. Then I got a box from Lillian Peterson in Mpls. She is another Smidths cousin, and in that box was, 2 box'es chocolat candy one box mixed candy, 1 cake, 2 package gum, 2 hersheys, a box of dates and nuts. Then I got a box of candy from Mrs. Wiberg. Then I got a package from the Red Cross and in it was a tablet, a package of envelops, 1 hankerchief, 1 pair woolen socks, 2 package gum 2 hersheys bars, 1 box mixed candy, a pipe, tobaca and cigeret papers. The tobaca I gave a way. And then I had that box from home. Say those wristlets [knitted mittens that leave the thumb and fingers exposed] are dandy. so you see I had all the eats I wanted. The other 7 boys in my tent got just as much eats so its funny we did not get sick eating so much. Well I will close this time with love to all

    Marland

★ ★ ★

Y.M.C.A.
"WITH THE COLORS"

[December 1917]

[The first two pages of this letter are missing.]

get court martialed. Did you read what Senator Knutsen put in the paper well thats true what he said.[7] I hope we get to some other camp soon. I heard they had a funeral for a captian in the next Regiment to day so you see officers are dieing as well. Those that dye are with pneumonia, spinal mengites. I have not heard of a fellow getting killed here yet, but there has been some awful close shaves. only last week, a couple hundred feet from where we were having band practise a sand pit caved in and three soldiers were caught under and all you could see of them was one fellows head. They were dug out as soon as possible. Two were taken to the Hospital they are all right now. So now don't worry over us atall. I only wish I was a cross the pond. So now be sure none of my let-

---

7. Marland probably refers to U.S. Representative Harold Knutson of Minnesota who, on December 11th, proposed a congressional resolution that would regulate the water levels of the Mississippi River and its tributaries.

ters get in the paper. [No information about camp military operations was to reach newspapers. Marland wrote "Do Not Publish" on some envelopes.]

received a letter to day from a lady in St. Paul and inside she enclosed a clipping what you put in some time ago. She did not sign her name to the letter so I don't know who she is. She also wrote a fine letter and beside sent an electric water heater. Which is very handy. She signed her Letter like this, An American woman (by naturatization) But now as board is concerned, we get eats and plenty of cloths. So now I think you will get a good idia of Camp Cody. Say the prices are awful high down here. They are regular robbers.

The 125th F. A. band was the only such mounted unit in the U.S. Army at this time.

Well I have some new news. We [the band] play on horse back now. What do you think of that. Its lot of fun to play on horse back. You auto seen the fellows when they seen us on horse back playing. We went past the colonels tent and he came out and started to jig, laugh, and ~~hot~~ hout and said we sure would soon go to France now

My Olga looks to have grown a lot taller and Jewel sure looks good Why didn't you and mamma get out there too. I can see mamma standing on the door step. She sure looks fine to. I am glad the camera caught her too. next time she wants to get out in good view. Them were sure good drawings. One thing you can feel good over pa and thats because the army is a better place for the fellow on this reason. Here they are kept away from boze They have to save at least ½ their wages and they learn to be a man. Here a fellow can't say I can't do that. But you have to do it when your told to or take the punishment of which I have not had any and don't expect to get any. So I think a year in the army does the fellows good. Well I don't know much more to write so I will close for this time With love to all

    Marland

    Now don't worry over me. Standly and I will be home after some time and every thing will be fine.

    Write soon.

Camp Cody, N.M.
Jan 3. 1918

Art Smith

Dear Sister + all,

    I received your most welcome letter to night and was sure glad to hear from you, only your letter was little short.

    I am feeling fine so please don't worry about me. I hop you are all the same. There has been an awful lot of pneumonia here. There are a few dieing every day.[8] I try and take the best of care of my self. I got some dandy cough medicine last night so I will fix the little cold I have alright. I believe the warm weather is beginning already. The day are quite hot already but its the nights that are so chilly. We got another blanket yesterday.

    I was up and saw Art. Smidt to night and I had a good time. [Probably Arthur E. Smith, one of the Svea boys] I go over to their street a couple times every week and see some of the fellows. Every thing is about the same so I realy don't know what to write about. New Years eve they had some dandy fire works here. We also had a fine supper. Thats about all we

8. Forty Camp Cody soldiers died at the base hospital from lobar pneumonia and measles related to pneumonia in the last four months of 1917. *Report of the Surgeon General of the Army, 1918,* (Washington: Government Printing Office, 1918) Table 46, 114.

had to remind us of N. Year. Have you heard from Standly lately. I see by the paper they are drilling and having a good time, so don't worry about him. I only wish I was with them. I hope we soon will be.

I got that box and every thing was jake [okay]. Thanks for it. Those things will come in very handy. Well as news is scarce I will close with love to all

Marland.

Write soon and make it a long one.

Camp Cody N.M
Jan 7. 1917 [1918]

Dear Sister + all,

I just received yours and papa letter and was sure glad to get it but it was so short. We had supper just a 1½ hour ago so I feel pretty good now. We had coffee, potatoes with peeling, vegtable sup, hash, peach sause and cake and bread for supper so you see that ain't bad.

I am feeling fine. Was up to the hospital yesterday and saw Roy Anderson he has rheumatism pretty bad. There are quiet a few that have that here. Pete Erickson is there too. He has ear and foot trouble, he is pretty bad. My the dust is blowing to day. We were supposed to have strecher drill but had first aid work so we did not need to go out in the dust.

We got are cannons to day. They got 24 of them. That makes 4 for each battery. They used the Iowa guns before, so they feel good we got are own now. [Conversion of the 34th Infantry Division to primarily an artillery outfit was proceeding slowly.]

We have brigade review every saterday. The review we had be fore the last one the

Marland photographed this American-made 3-inch field gun used for training. The light 800-pound piece fired 3-inch-caliber 15-pound shells and had an effective range of nearly four miles.

band played for 35 mineuts with out stopping so you see it is not so easy some times. How would you like to play some hard music for 35 mineuts with out stopping I think you would get a little tired. Have you heard any thing from Standley yet I have not [Marland's brother had been in France with Minnesota's 151st Field Artillery since November.] Well everything is the same about only we are getting more work all the time.

I bet you are having a good time costing [coasting]. I wish I could help Jewel diliver [groceries] a little I bet she gets tired some times. I don't blame her. I am glad papa has such good trade. Say you want to be sure and get a small picture of the store. I sure am anxious my self. I am glad to hear Lesile [Wiberg, a Trenton neighbor] liked it. I bet pa is sure glad he got out of Svea. Say have they got a rule on selling sugar Like only a certain amount to each one. How does mamma like her new stove. Has pa got a furnace in the celler write a big letter on the house and so on. I would like to hear all about it. Any little news is welcome. Well I don't know much more to write about. Say to tell pa to drop Albin a line him self. His address is "Bat. B. 125 U.S.F.A." So I will close this time with Love to all.

Marland.

Now write a big long letter real soon.

The Red Wing-Trenton Connection

There is good reason that reference to Red Wing, Minnesota, appears in the letters of the Williams brothers, two men brought up near Hager City in the Town of Trenton, Wisconsin. Hager and Trenton are directly across the Mississippi River from Red Wing, a city of about 9,000 in 1918. Small Wisconsin towns, including Hager City, were linked to the mini-metropolis of Red Wing by a wagon bridge in 1895. Prior to that structure, ferryboats and cable ferries connected Trenton and Red Wing.

A busy riverport since its 1857 founding, Red Wing developed into an industrial and agricultural hub with abundant jobs in its numerous factories and busy retail districts. Wisconsin residents often worked and shopped in the Minnesota city. They still do today.

The Williams home near Hager was just six miles from Red Wing.

Marland Williams, while a student at Red Wing Seminary

Marland and Stanley attended Red Wing Seminary, founded 1879. It featured Junior College, Theological, Commercial, and Academy departments. When Marland's Duluth-based National Guard company—the reason he enlisted there has been lost—entrained for Camp Cody, other units, including Red Wing's Company L, joined them. Marland quickly made contact with his former friends from Wisconsin and Red Wing.

An important but little remembered military connection exists between the future Great War soldiers living in Wisconsin in 1917 and their Red Wing comrades. At least twenty Pierce County, Wisconsin, men crossed the river at Red Wing to enroll in Company L of the Minnesota National Guard, a major contribution to an outfit typically of about 100 soldiers. Marland mentions a number of these men in his letters, particularly those who came from the area around Svea Lutheran Church in Hager City.[9] [See footnote for a list of Wisconsin soldiers in Company L.]

Camp Cody, N.M.
Jan 13. 1918

Dear Folks.

Six months ago to day I left for Duluth. It don't seem like that long. Well I am feeling fine. I got a little cold but I just went over to get some cough medicine and it sure tast fine not.

I got a letter from Sidney to night and he told all about what they did at Svea Xmas. [Sidney Peterson was Marland's first cousin who lived in the Svea area.]

We had another brigade review yesterday. It sure looks fine to see 6000 soldiers lined up for review

Every thing is about the same here. We had a little snow the other morning but it did not last long. The mountains sure looked pretty that morning to the see the snow on them and their peaks hidden in the cloud.

Have you heard from Standly I have not. we put up some more

9. *Goodhue County in the World War* (Red Wing: Red Wing Printing, 1919) 186–187. Photos of soldiers from Company L are provided. *Pierce County in the World War* (Red Wing: Red Wing Printing, 1919). Photographs of soldiers include Wisconsin men and their enlistment dates in Red Wing's Company L. Pierce County, Wisconsin, men enlisted in Red Wing's Company L include John C. Brown, Gottfred and Arthur Hullander, Chester W. Irvine, Theodore Peterson, Lyle V. Strothman, Albin O. Gustafson, Arthur E. Smith, Harold Sharp, Albert Flynn, Lloyd J. Taggart, Frank Bach, Arthur M. Olson, Francis S. Roach, Irvine Benson, Clifford E. Kish, Roy E. McKeen, Eugene Nadeau, Ludwig Anderson, and Carl E. Sundell. *Note:* The Red Wing–Trenton connection relates directly to historiographer Johnson's family. His maternal grandparents were born on the Wisconsin side of the Mississippi; they later moved to Red Wing where they met. Johnson's grandmother was a first cousin of the two Hullander brothers from Trenton who joined Company L.

tents and there are only going to be 5 in a tent after this. So we will have a little more room. It rain a little to day. The rain we got wensday was the first we had for 3 months and 7 days. I will have to do like olga says will write more later

Marland.

The 34th Sandstorm Division passes in review at Camp Cody.

Camp Cody
Jan 20 1918

Dear Papa + all.

Will write you a few lines to night and let you know I am feeling fine. You don't want to worry over me as I try to take the best care I can of my self. Pete Erickson is not dead. He was feeling pretty good to day and Arthur Hullander is getting better.[10]

The doctors at the base hospital are as good as one can get and they also do all they possibly can do for one. Those that have pneumonia the[y] tape [tap] the lungs and even put silver tubes in the lungs so they will drain.[11] The[y] took 2 pints of blood out of Arthur Hullander and pumped his lung twice. So you see the doctors are all right They have 3 lady nurses in each ward to. The Red Cross is sure great if you can help them any always do it because

10. Pvt. Arthur Hullander was a friend from Svea Lutheran Church near Hager City, Wisconsin, Svea Lutheran Church records. Hullander was born June 18, 1896, in Pierce County, Wisconsin. He joined Red Wing's National Guard Co. L and was discharged for disability in March 1918, FindaGrave.com.

11. Physicians at Camp Cody and elsewhere used surgery in attempting to drain the pus-filled space between the two thin membranes surrounding the lungs. They hoped to ease breathing or prevent more severe infection. The surgery typically collapsed one lung, sometimes both. Gillett reports, "At some camps mortality following early operation ran as high as 90 percent." Mary C. Gillett, *The Army Medical Department*, 1917–1941 (Washington D.C.: GPO, 1981) 157–159.

THE
Song of Camp Cody

BY F. B. CAMP

Dedicated to the Soldiers of the 34th Division U. S. Army, Located at Deming, New Mexico

Camp Cody, Camp Cody, where the sun is hot and bright,
Where the moon is always shining, through the cooler hours of night,
Where the Gila monster warbles to the moon with keener sight,
And the bloomin' "Centipedus," fill our souls with awful fright.

Where the horned toad and the lizard, flourish like the mesquite tree,
Where the ever present tarantula, keeps you watching constantly,
Where the soldier, in his anguish, does a frenzied song and dance,
When a scorpion jabs his stinger through the bosom of his pants.

Where the everlasting cactus stabs you with its renowned thorn,
Where the sizzling heat of summer makes you look on clothes with scorn,
Where the army mule and burro, sing in pleasing harmony,
And the bugler blowing "Pay Day," fills your restless soul with glee.

Where the roar and whirr of autos, can be heard both night and day,
Where the whistling, seething sand storm drives your peace of mind away,
Where the dust from gentle zephyrs, fills your eyes and nose and ears,
And the scorching sun, while drilling, quickly dries the threatened tears.

Where the camp is "Dry" as tinder, and you cannot drown your thirst,
Though you drink of pop and Bone-dry, 'till you very nearly burst,
Where the ice cream cone and candy, fill the company canteen,
And they sometimes feed you "Willie" with the staple army bean.

Where they charge a quarter dollar, from the camp to Deming town,
Where you go to see the Ducklings, that have lost their youth and down,
Where they take your hard-earned dollar and never bat an eye,
Though you look at it quite tearful, as you kiss the plunk goodbye.

Where our dearly lov-ed regiments that used to be the Guards,
Disappeared entirely when they shuffled up the cards,
Where the Hundred Odd Battalion, of Bombadiers and "Gats,"
Was organized one morning, from a dozen Border frats.

Where we drill from morn 'till evening, and dream we drill at night,
Where they're making us all ready, for the big and final fight,
Where we get the daily letter from the loved ones at home,
And the rudiments of dicipline are sifting through your dome.

Where the Y's have movie pictures, and the chaplains entertain,
Where the crap game and the barber never fail to make a gain,
Where everybody's happy as they learn to play the game,
Oh! we love you, Camp Cody, yes, we love you just the same.

So here's to you, Camp Cody, and all your soldier men,
We are living in your confines, twenty thousand men and ten,
We are drilling and we're waiting, and we're game to take a chance,
With the rest of Uncle's soldiers on the battlefields of France.

what they do is for the good of the sick and us fellows. Whats gets the fellows here is the light dry air and dust Thats what so hard on the pneumonia cases. Every thing is about the same here. So there is not much to write about. Say next time you write give me the address you write to standly with. I have wrote him a number of letters. I only wish we were across now. I made quiet a mistake when I did not join his Rigement. Well we have to live and learn. I will have a lot to tell about when I get home. I sure have learnt many things sent [since] in the army. One thing we all no [is] that

Filling mattress ticks with straw

we will appreciate home more when we get back. My it will seem funny to stay in a house again. I have not been in a house since we left Duluth. I like are army cots fine. We have a straw mattress and four woolen blankets so we keep warm. The air is so funny here when its cold nothing will keep a fellow warm the chill seems to go right throu.[12] Well its bed time and I guess I will close for this time, with love to all

 Marland

I saw Albin G. [Gustafson, another Trenton soldier from Red Wing's Co. L] yesterday and hes feeling fine. Write soon

★ ★ ★

Deming N.M.
Jan 22 1918

Dear Sister + All.

Will write you a few lines and let you know I am feeling fine.

We have regular winter weather here now. We had a couple inches of snow day before yesterday but its almost gone now. Its a good thing it snows a little as it makes the air a lot fresher and settles the dust. This morning about 5 oclock we heard the bugle blow fire call, and we all jumped up as that is our orders and when

---

12. The men lived eight to a tent. Most tents later had wood-burning stoves and a single electric light. C. A. Gustafson, "Inside Camp Cody," *Desert Winds Magazine*, 5/10 (Nov. 1992) not paginated.

we got up we saw that the base hospital was on fire. The captain ordered all of us to take our blankets a long so if the patients had to be moved we could give them our blankets to keep warm. But lucky it was the nurses quarters that burnt. They soon got the fire out. This hospital is the largest one U.S. has got, so you see if there had been a good wind we would have had some time.

Two members of the base fire department

Well every thing is about the same. Its kind of hard playing out in the snow now as our instruments freeze up. We got a new stove in our tent so we have it quiet warm now. It seems funny to saw in a tent all winter but I like it. Say have you forgot how to write I have not heard from home for a week now. Well its 10 oclock and as I feel kind of tired I will go to bed now. I wish I could go in the pantry and get a little lunch before I went to bed. I bet Pa is doing that him self now.

With love to all
Marland
Have not heard from Standly.

★ ★ ★

Camp Cody. NM
Jan 27 1918

Dear papa + all.

I received Olgas and mammas letters yesterday. Glad to hear you are all well. Hope Olgas throat will get well soon. I am feeling fine. I was up to the Hospital to see Arthur Hullander. He has pneumonia. He past the worst yesterday so I guess he will pull throu allright. He was so bad that they telegraphed his folks that they thought he would not live so Fred H. came down. [Probably Carl Frederick Hullander, Arthur's older brother.] He got here this morning. I talked with him this after noon. Its pretty nice to see some one from up north.

Pete Erickson also has pneumonia. I don't know if he will pull though or not. Miss Jerdeen [Christine Girdeen of Trenton] you know the one he went with came down here yesterday to [take] care of him.[13] He had some ear and foot trouble, so hes been in the Hospital 3 months so he was pretty weak. I also saw one of are band boys in the Hospital to day he has pneumonia but hes almost ready to get out of the hospital now.

The doctors are pretty good here now. I suppose you remember Roy Anderson of Red Wing [Company L] Hes at the Hospital too he has rheumatism. He is just getting so he can walk around now. I suppose you heard a lot about that insurance.[14] Well I took out $10,000 [$158,945]. It is best I tell you all about it in case anything should happen you no what to expect. In case of death the benafishury will receive $57.50 [$912] amonth for 240 months. It cost me $6.40 [$102] a month so thats cheap. Just about every one takes this insurance. and if a person is wounded he will received according to his injurie They will do that now instead of give [a] pension.

Its rained quiet abit lately. It was to bad we had so nice weather when governor Burnquist was here.[15] I don't believe we ever had such good weather as when he was here. Else every thing is about the same.

I suppose prices are getting pretty high up there. I wish I could help you a little but I guess we will have to Wait a <u>little</u> while yet.

They changed our tents so we are only five in a tent now makes it pretty nice. We are only four in are tent as the fellow that has pneumonia is in our tent and he wont be back for 6 weeks yet.

Say I have wrote a number of letters to standley its funny He did not get them.

Well I will close this time with love to All
Marland.

---

13. Fred Hullander, of the Town of Trenton, was Arthur's older brother.

14. Congress funded the War Risk insurance program in 1917 that protected soldiers from the hazards of war.

15. Joseph A. A. Burnquist served as Minnesota's governor during World War I, a contentious time in state history. With the legislature not in session, lawmakers placed the Commission of Public Safety, chaired by Burnquist, in power. The CPS task: suppress anti-war movements and pro-German activity in the state. The commission proved very aggressive, producing complaints from around the state that citizens' constitutional rights were being violated. William Watts Folwell, *A History of Minnesota* (St. Paul: Minnesota Historical Society, 1969 edition) 3: 557. Folwell provides a concise history of the Minnesota Commission of Public Safety in Appendix 19, 3: 556–575.

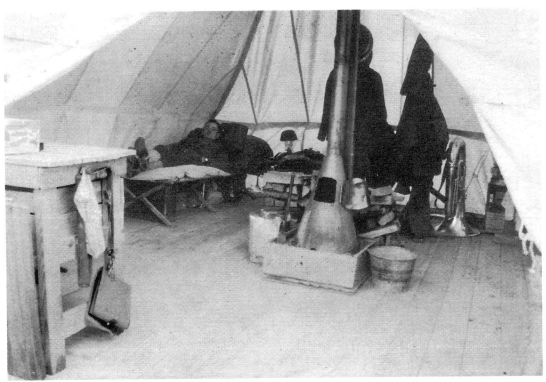

Interior view of Marland's tent. Note the wood-burning stove and tuba.

Camp Cody. N.M
Feb. 1 1918

Dear Folks + all.

Will write you a few lines and let you know I am feeling fine. I got that box yesterday. Thanks It sure was fine. I got a bottle of milk to night, so I will have a regular old lunch to night.

We had a good time to night. We played at are regimental hall and they had a few movies. I [am] trying to write lying on my cot as some of the fellows are using the table so its [a] little hard writing. we were playing on horse back to day. Had a lot of fun. They are kind of short of horses so we can not all ways get are old horse. It hard to take a new horse out because they get scared of the horns. I like to see you ride [one] of these horse. I see Gov. Burndquist put quiet a piece in the paper. I would be glad if we were moved to some other camp. It is starting to get warmer all ready. I suppose it has started to melt a little up there to. I have heard nothing from

Standley. I wrote him one day before yesterday. When you write him tell I have wrote him a number of times. I only hope we can get a cross. After we have gone this far I think we auto go the rest of the way. The batteries are comeing along pretty fast now with their drilling. You auto see them lay telephone wire. The wire is on a two wheel cart hitched to two horse and they sure go. Then a few fellows on horse back come with the phones and conect them and in only a few mineuts a few miles of telephone is layed. They also have a big wireless station in our company they can receive messages from St Paul on it. They are not allowed to use it yet as they have not received their papers on it. I can hear the fire whistle blow up in Deming now. I suppose some mud shack or candy stand is burning.

Well I will close this time with love to all
Marland.
Art Hullander is better and so it Pete E. Thanks for that box

[Envelope with a three-cent stamp addressed to Miss Olga Williams, 391 Arundel St, St. Paul, Minn.; "Do not publish in part or whole" handwritten at the top on the back.]

125TH FIELD ARTILLERY BAND
CAMP CODY, NEW MEXICO

Feb 13, 1918

Dear Sister + All.

Will write you a few lines and let you know I am feeling fine. I hope you are all the same. The weather is about the same as changeable as always. We played for a funeral to day and one yesterday. That makes our fifth one.[16] One was from Bat. E and one was from the medical Detachment. But [both] died of pneumonia.

16. Patty Israel, a Deming resident at this time, told about military funerals. "The soldiers and the band would come down Pine [Street] with caisson and casket in their funeral march to the railroad station to put the body on the train…. Some people were disturbed when the band would play a cheerful tune on the way back. They considered it a sort of sacrilege." C. A. Gustafson, "A Silent Enemy," *Desert Winds Magazine*, 5/10 (Nov. 1992) not paginated.

One more fellow in the band has pneumonia, so I hope we will get moved out of here pretty soon. Its too bad about those that were sunk on that boat wasn't it.[17]

I suppose you and Jewel are going to school all the time. Glad to hear you like your new teacher better. I believe I mentioned we were quarnteened with the measles and will be yet for some time. In one way I don't care. We got out of 3 concerts sunday on account of it.

Arthur and Pete are geting better. Two more Red Wing boys have pneumonia. They are Holter and C. Asp. Now I don't want to have you worry over me, as I take the best care over myself, but I will be glad when we move out

The 125th F. A. Band played in formation for a soldier's funeral, Deming, New Mexico.

Now I don't want none of this told around as they are awful strict about our writing. I have not heard from Standly. As you know it takes a long time for his letters to come across so don't worry over him. I only wish he could of got a many letters and boxes as I got from home but as he is across the pound I know its hard for him to get all the mail. It will be nice when the war is over when we both can come home again. It sure would seem funny to come in a house and set down to a table where one can use plates and help him self to things and then don't need to wash his own dishes every meal. And then to think of sleeping in a nice bed. It don't seem as oh it was in August that I last was in a house.

Well news is scarce, so I will close for this time with love to All Marland

now don't worry and write soon

17. Marland is probably referring to the sinking of the SS *Tuscania*, a luxury ocean liner that was converted to a troopship. On February 5, 1918, *Tuscania* was transporting American soldiers across the Atlantic when it was torpedoed by a German U-boat and sunk off the north coast of Ireland. While 2,187 soldiers were rescued, 166 American and 44 British lives were lost. Martin Gilbert, *The First World War, A Complete History* (New York: Henry Holt and Co., 1994) 328-329, 397.

★ ★ ★

[Envelope with a three-cent stamp addressed to Mr. Alvin Williams, 391 Arundel St, St. Paul, Minn.; "Do not Publish in Part or Whole" handwritten on the left margin.]

125ᵀᴴ Field Artillery Band
Camp Cody, New Mexico

Sun Feb. 17. 1918

Dear Papa + Mamma + All.

I received your most welcome letter to night, and was sure glad to hear you are all well. I am feeling fine too. I am kind of tired to night as we worked quiet hard to day altho it was Sun. I will write you a few lines any way. I suppose you would like to know what I did that we get tired. Well first we played reveale, Then we play for church. After that we walked to to the base Hospital and gave a concert to the sick. After The concert I went to see some of the fellows. I saw Arthur Hullander, Harold Sharpe [and] Roy anderson.[18] They are quiet well now. We have a fellow from the band there with pneumonia hes quiet sick.

Marland reading a book

Then after dinner we went down to the stadium and give an other concert. I will in close a program of this. All the bands played to gather in this program. Then after that we played retreat so you see we are quiet busy. After supper I finished a book entitled (When a Man's a Man) [a fictional account of ranch life in Arizona by Harold Bell Wright published in 1916]. I think you have read it. If not you auto. To morrow we play for another funeral one of the Leutenents died of pneumonia.

18. Several of Marland's friends joined Red Wing's National Guard Company L: Arthur Hullander and Harold Sharpe were from Trenton, Wisconsin. "Svea boys" Albin Gustafson and Arthur E. Smith were from nearby Hager City and Bay City, Wisconsin. Roy Anderson lived in Red Wing.

I see some of the svea boys quiet often. I see Albin G. [Gustafson] Loyd T. Goutfred [Gotfried] [and] Art Smith.[19] and some of them every day as we go by their street a couple time a day. I see Albert quite often too. He has payed me. Chester is not in our Regiment I have not seen him for a couple months. Hes in the Machine Gun Reg. Pete E is geting better. The Chaplin said if it had not been for Christen Gerdeen coming down he would have been a dead boy. She is here yet.

There now I guess that answers most of your questions. I got Albins letter too. I will take it over to morrow. Now I suppose you wonder what [I] am am doing with the big salery I am getting. Well they take $20 [$375] a month for L. bonds[20] Then $6.40 [$120] for insurance. Then I get the big sum of $9.60 [$180] for myself and the law requires we keep not less than $7.50 [$140] so you see I spend an awful lot of money. Just think I have taken in one show down town since we came to Camp. so you see I spend a lot of money don't I. But than there a lot of little things we have to get and that counts up. Well I am trying to do my best and thats all you expect I am sure. And I know Standley is doing the same.

Say I got a letter from Rev. Grant of the F.L. Church [First Lutheran Church, 463 Maria Avenue, St. Paul] wanting me to join it. He said Standley had been there a number of times and that he had all so saw you and ma there. Now I don't know him or ever been to his church so I do not know what to answer him. I dont even [know] what church you belong too now. But if you join that church I surley would want you to put down my name. But what I want is this. I want to belong to the church you and mamma belong long too because I know you will chose correctly. So please let me know a bout this.

You say you think Standleys girl is pretty nice. Glad to hear it. I knew you would like what he picked out because if I may use this

19. Albin O. Gustafson was born July 28, 1894, and died November 30, 1928. He is buried in Svea Lutheran Cemetery in the Town of Trenton, Pierce County, Wisconsin. FindaGrave.com.

20. Creation and sale of Liberty Bonds is credited largely to U.S. Secretary of the Treasury William McAdoo. He designed the program to help finance the war and create active citizen involvement in the war effort. Americans purchased $17 billion in bonds by war's end. Highly advertised bond drives, in some cases, were conducted with a zealousness that bordered upon coercion. But twenty million individuals bought bonds at a time when the nation had only 24 million households. For a detailed essay on the bond sale effort see http://www.federalreservehistory.org/Events/DetailView/100, "Liberty Bonds."

—: PROGRAM :—

"AMERICA,"
Sung by the Division Chorus of Five Hundred Voices.

MARCH.
"The Blue Flag," - - - - - - - *Carrie Jacob Bond.*
(Dedicated to the 21st. U. S. Infantry.)

OVERTURE.
"Undine," - - - - - - - , - - - *Lortzing.*

SUITE :
"Don Quixote," - - - - - - - - - *Safranek.*

No. 1 (A Spanish Village.)   No. 3 (Dulcinea)
No. 2 (Sancho Panza)   No. 4 (Don Quixote.)

This Suite is founded on the story of the same name by Cervantes, and of the four parts, the first three are characteristic. The fourth is somewhat descriptive, introducing the Don's warlike but sad nature. During his journey in quest of adventure he discovers the windmills. After the encounter he again set forth, lamely at first, but eventually is again the self-confident, heroically-inclined knight of yore.

a. Fantasia, "The Warrior's Return," - - - - - *Kuchen*
Synopsis : (In the distance ; Approaching ; Arrival ;
Soldier Chorus ; People's Rejoicing ; Prayer)

b. Intermezz, "Agnus Dei," - - - - - - - *Bizet*

Selection, "I Lombardi," - - - - - - - *Verdi*

"STAR SPANGLED BANNER," (Sung by Div. Chorus of 500 Voices)

JACOB SCHMIDT,
Division Band Leader

HERMAN FRENGER, Y. M. C. A.,
Chorus Director.

BAND PROGRAM
FEBRUARY 17, 1918

Marland and the 125th Field Artillery band were kept busy with daily morning marches through camp, formal military functions, practice, funerals, and concerts in Deming with programs such as the one shown here. The Division Chorus of 500 men sang "America" and "The Star Spangled Banner." The program omitted the word "The" from "The Star Spangled Banner."

AMERICA
My county 'tis of thee,
Sweet land of liberty,
Of thee I sing;
Land where my fathers died,
Land of the pilgrim's pride;
From ev'ry mountain side
Let freedom ring!

Our fathers' God to Thee,
Author of liberty,
To Thee we sing:
Long may our land be bright
With freedom's holy light;
Protect us by Thy might,
Great God, our King!

STAR SPANGLED BANNER
Oh, thus be it ever when freeman shall stand
Between their loved homes and the war's desolation
Blest with victory and peace, may the heav'n-rescued land
Praise the Pow'r that hath made and preserved us a nation.
Then conquer we must, when our cause it is just,
And this be our motto: "In God is our trust!"
And the Star Spangled Banner in triumph shall wave
O'er the land of the free and the home of the brave!

"The Star Spangled Banner" did not become the official national anthem until 1931, but under a decree by President Wilson, was used as such during the Great War. The words provided in music programs were often those of the fourth verse, rather than the first, familiar to us.

expression (Hes a chip off the old block.) Well you don't need to worry over me as I have did no hunting yet. I guess I will have to wait till after the war as there is nothing in Camp Cody. I guess I will have to get dry behind the ears first as you used to say.

Glad to hear you and the rest are having a good time. I guess I will have my share when I get home. To be home a gain will be pleasure enough for me.

I guess I am forgetting to quiet. Well you asked for a long letter. Will this do. Did you get those pictures I sent. Well I will close this time with love to all

Marland

Now Dady I will be waiting for a quick long answer on this letter.

Say Olga asked why I wrote (Do not publish in whole or part.) Thats a law in camp here so the people wont put anything what we write in the papers. If we do not put that on, the letters are subject to censorship. See

A Woman of Courage

A soldier's death from disease is no less tragic to family and friends than the loss of a life in battle. The story of Christine Girdeen [Marland spelled her surname various ways] illustrates an admirable and determined woman's attempt to save the soldier she loved.

Christine Girdeen reviewed her options in early January 1918. She had learned that her sweetheart, Pvt. Peter A. Erickson, was dangerously ill at Camp Cody, New Mexico. Girdeen and Erickson lived in Trenton, Wisconsin, before being separated by the Great War. Marland Williams, who knew them both, had reported in a January 7, 1918, letter to his family that Pvt. Erickson was dangerously ill. Then, good news from Marland arrived on January 27. "Miss Jerdeen, you know the one he went with," had arrived at Camp Cody to "take care of [Pete]."[21]

Twenty-three-year-old Christine Girdeen may have been among the American women liberating themselves from Victorian codes of "lady-like" behavior. She might have made the arduous journey from Wisconsin to Deming, New Mexico, unescorted, although it is possible she traveled with Fred Hullander, a Trenton man who also came to Camp Cody

21. Marland paid close attention to the well-being of his many Trenton area friends stationed at Camp Cody. He mentioned Peter Erickson's struggle to survive illness in seven letters (January 7, 27; February 1, 13, 17, 23). C. A. Gustafson, "Inside Camp Cody," *Desert Winds Magazine*, 8 (November 1995) accessed November 27, 2016. http://demingnewmexico.genealogyvillage.com/CampCody/hst04.htm.

at this time. With the military's approval or acquiescence, the Trenton woman reached a base of some 25,000 soldiers where death by disease was not uncommon. She was prepared to nurse the man she had dated back to health.

Remarkably, Pete Erickson rallied under Christine's care. Wrote Marland on February 17, "The Chaplin said if it had not been for Christen Gerdeen coming down he would have been a dead boy. She is here yet."

Marland wrote a somber end to this story on February 23. "We played for Pete Erickson's funeral yesterday. My but he had fallen off. You would not have known him if you saw him. Miss Gerdeen went home with the body yesterday…. The government paid [her] fare home as she had charge of the body…. It was sure great of her to stay and take care of Pete."

Christine lived in Trenton until 1922 when she married Daniel M. Olander. The Olanders moved to Goodhue County's Belle Creek Township, ten miles southwest of Red Wing. She died in Hager City, Wisconsin, on October 2, 1965.

[Envelope with a three-cent stamp addressed to Miss Olga Williams, 391 Arundel St, St. Paul, Minn.; "Do not Publish" handwritten on the left margin.]

125ᵀᴴ Field Artillery Band
Camp Cody, New Mexico

Feb. 23–1918

Dear Sister + all

Received your letter yesterday glad to hear you are all well. Well I am the same as always. We just had breakfeast. My but it warm this morning it must be about 75° now. It was near a hundred yesterday. We played for Pete Ericksons funeral yesterday.[22] My but he had fallen off. you would not know him if you saw him. Miss Gerdeen went home with the body yesterday. Roy Anderson (Red Wing) also went with home. He got a discharge for Rheumatism. The government paid miss Gerdeens fare home as she had charge of the body. The company took up a collection for $65 dollars [$1,218.75] and gave her to. It sure was great of her to stay and take care of Pete. Its no fun to be in a hospital all alone when you are as sick

---

22. Private Peter A. Erickson was born in 1890 and died in 1918 while at Camp Cody. He is buried in Bethlehem Lutheran Cemetery in the Town of Trenton, Pierce County, Wisconsin, FindAGrave.com.

as he was. He is realy better off the way he went as he would have been a cripple. they oppereated 8 times on him. and then he had ear trouble, and Rheumatism so bad.

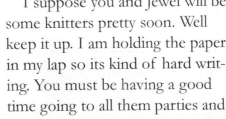

Hearses brought bodies to Deming for burial or transport back home.

You said it looked funny to see the mountains so close. Well the closest one you see is 15 miles away. That high peak you see is 35 miles away.

I suppose you and Jewel will be some knitters pretty soon. Well keep it up. I am holding the paper in my lap so its kind of hard writing. You must be having a good time going to all them parties and so on. Tell pa that Sorenson was up and seen me yesterday hes a nice little fellow.

Well the mail mans coming so I will have to close with love to all

Marland

Write soon

★ ★ ★

[Envelope with a three-cent stamp addressed to Mr. Alvin Williams, 391 Arundel St, St. Paul, Minn.; "Do not Publish" handwritten on the left margin.]

125ᵀᴴ FIELD ARTILLERY BAND
CAMP CODY, NEW MEXICO

Feb. 24—19-18

Dear Father + All.

Received your letter and was glad to receive it. Don't think, I will ever get tiried reading your letters. I am always looking for mail from home. I am feeling fine, and hope you are all the same. We sure got some swell weather now. We go in our shirt sleves from when we get up till we go to bed, so its a little different then 20° below.

We played another funeral saterday. It was a fellow from the remount.[23] He was thrown off a mule and his foot caught in the stirrup and dragged which killed him.

The railroad tracks leading to camp were lined with hay bales to feed as many as 10,000 horses.

I hear we are going out to the gun range soon so if we go there I might not be able to write for a week so if you do not get any mail don't worry. I have not heard from Standley but don't worry about him. The mail service is held up so, that its hard to get mail through. Every thing is about the same here. I heard to night we might leave pretty soon for France, but am not sure, so don't say anything about it.

I hear from Sidney quiet often, and hes always the same to me. I don't suppose he knows just what to write Olga so that why may be he don't write. I suppose thats all you hear is war up there. I bet the sinking of that transport awakened them up a little. News is scarce to night and I don't know nothing to write about, so I will close this time

With love to all

Marland

I enclose a program we played Sunday

★ ★ ★

125ᵗʰ Field Artillery Band
Camp Cody, New Mexico

Mar. 1. 1918

Dear Sister + All.

Received your letter Thur. So I guess it's time to answer. I am feeling fine, and hope you are all well. Its been a nasty day to day. It snowed almost all fornoon. But its all melted now

23. The remount station in the northern part of Camp Cody was equipped to handle 10,000 horses and mules. This 100-acre area included a huge loading platform, corrals, a veterinary hospital, and a horseshoeing school. http://demingnewmexico.genealogyvillage.com/index.html#life. A report illustrates the need for fodder for the animals: "Mountains of baled hay, piled 52 high, were stacked along the [railroad] tracks." C. A. Gustafson, "Inside Camp Cody," *Desert Winds Magazine*, 8 (November 1995) not paginated.

Winters in the high desert around camp may have reminded Upper Midwestern soldiers of home.

I had a letter from Sidney Thur. and one from Leslie Wiberg yesterday. So Uncle Ed bought [the] Ed. Samulson place.[24] I wonder if he is going to get married.

I suppose you know Gust Andrews is dead he died this week.

So you said mamma was going to put that tray Papa got away till you had a new house. well thats good news. I only wish I had some money to give pa [to] buy a house with but tell him that in July I will have $200.⁰⁰ [$3,178] in Liberty bonds. He can figure on that if its worth using. I just took out those plans you sent me a long time ago and was wondering how you had room to live over the store. I wont hardly be room when Standley and I get back will it.

So you don't practise Rag time. Well it wont hurt you to play it some. We play a lot of it in the band. It wont hurt you. But Clasical music is best and I am glad to see you take and interest in it. Does Jewel play any. You auto get her started a little too. It will help her a lot. I suppose Papa hammers a way as usual. Well news is scarce so will cloths close. With Love to all

Marland

I wrote Rev Grant. Have you heard from Standley. A fellow here got a letter from one in his bunch and he says they are all fine.

24. Ed Peterson was a younger brother to Marland's father, Alvin. He was among the five Peterson siblings who did not change their surname to Williams. The Samuelson farm was in the Town of Trenton, Pierce County, Wisconsin. Ed never married.

★ ★ ★

125ᵀᴴ FIELD ARTILLERY BAND
CAMP CODY, NEW MEXICO

Mar. 4, 1918

Dear Sister + All

Will write you a few lines to night and let you know I am feeling fine I have had no letter from you's for some time but I hope you are all the same. We played a concert at the base hospital to night for the sick. To morrow night we play at the Y. So you see we are kept busy. I will inclose a program of last Sundays concert.

Every thing is about the same. Its getting a little warmer now. I suppose you are biggening to feel spring up there too.

I suppose you will soon be confirmed. I bet you will be glad when your thro, as you wont have to study so hard then.

The YMCA was one of the few permanent buildings at Camp Cody, largely a tent city.

Say did you ever have any more pictures taken. I will be glad to see them if you do, as you know a picture says a lot more than a letter. when you have some more taken, get ma + pa on it to. I don't think you are as fat so you will cover the whole picture your self. I did not mean to for get darling Jewel. Besure to get the store on them. I bet you are getting a little high toned, going to so many parties and so on. Well have a good time and one for me too.

Well news is scarce to night and as I am a little tired I will fix my cot and go to bed. It would seem funny to crawl in and not need to make my bed. Well It will be some time before I can do that. I like the cots now. We have four woolen blankets so we keep good and warm.

Well good night to you all
Marland.

Tell Mamma I am short of towels and if she has a couple extra I can make good use of them. One or two bath towels would be handy to. You see we have to wash a lot as it is so dusty.

★ ★ ★

125ᵀᴴ FIELD ARTILLERY BAND
CAMP CODY, NEW MEXICO

Mar. 9. 1918

Dear Papa + All.

Will answer your letter which I received Thur. I am feeling fine as always. My its warm to day. We had a division review for Sec. of War Baker to-day, and we had to walk about ten miles.[25] We were the first band to pass the reviewing office[r]s to day so we had to march and play half a mile with out stopping at 130 steps a mineut so you see we sure were sweting when we got throu.

I was in our sergents tent to day and he showed me two Letters he got from a fellow yesterday that is in the 151ˢᵗ F.A. He says everything is fine. So don't worry over Standely. I know he will take good care of himself. I only wished I had joined that Reg. so we could of been to gather. [While Marland yearned to be in France with his brother, Stanley was writing to him to "stay where he is." See Stanley's letter of April 14.]

Say what makes you think F.H. borrowed money from me. He never asked me for any, and I would not of had any to have lent him.

No, Christin [Christine Girdeen] does not get any of Petes insurance. He had ten thousand [dollars of] insurance and it all goes to his mother. $57.50 [$914] a month for twenty years or with interest that makes $13,800 [$219,344].

The 125ᵗʰ Field Artillery band, shown on parade, awakened Camp Cody each morning at 5:30.

That the same as I have got. You see that insurance goes to the nearest relative in the family or so on but no one out side of the relation can get it.

25. Newton Diehl Baker (1871-1937) served as President Woodrow Wilson's Secretary of War from March 1916 to March 4, 1921. He was educated at Johns Hopkins University and received a law degree from Washington and Lee University. William Gardner Bell, *Secretaries of War and Secretaries of the Army* (Washington D.C.: Center of Military History, U.S. Army, 1992) 112, http://www.history.army.mil/books/Sw-SA/Baker.html.

You did not say what church you put my name in but I suppose its the one your going to join. I bet your glad its getting warmer again. The grass is nice and green down here now. but there is very little of it, as only a few civilians have planted it in their yards.

I had a letter from Bunny yesterday. I had a bath a few mineuts a go and I feel a little lazy now, and as news is scarce, I will close this time With Love to all,

Marland

Write soon

We play another funeral yesterday a fellow in the engineers died

Soldiers washing up at day's end

★ ★ ★

125TH FIELD ARTILLERY BAND
CAMP CODY, NEW MEXICO

Sun. [Mar.] 10, 1918

Dear Father + all.

I just received your letter glad to see Standleys too. We played church over for the enguneers Reg. this morning. My its fine out now. The sun is pretty hot.

I am glad Standely likes it over there. When he sends some pictures over send them down here so I can see them will you. I will send them right back.

Glad to see you got such grat trade. So you have the moving fever again have you. I thought you could not stay on a place long.

I wish it was dinner now. I am getting a little hungry. we have to play another

This large tent served as the band's rehearsal space.

concert this after noon. I will send you a program latter. I don't know if you care to see them, but by reading them you can see what kind of music we play.

It would be kind of nice if I could keep up music after I come home. I have learnt quiet a bit, but I have a lot to learn yet.

We might go out to the range to morrow. Its out by the mountains. The fellows like it fine there. It will be a little change. All the boys are feeling fine.

I will close this time, Love to All.

Marland

Just because you and Olga write a letter to gather It don't count for too.

[Envelope with a three-cent stamp, addressed to Mr. Alvin Williams, 391 Arundel St, St. Paul, Minn.; "Do not Publish" handwritten on left margin.]

125TH FIELD ARTILLERY BAND
CAMP CODY, NEW MEXICO

Mar. 14, 1918

Dearest Folks.

Will write you a few lines to night and let you know I am feeling better than ever. I received your package to night. I did not mean you should send so much. That cake sure is swell. Ill have soap for some time now. But it takes a lot to keep clean here. My but the sand has blown these last two days.

I got Olga's letter this after noon. I hope there is some thing in what she said, about us moving. But we hear so many stories. We don't believe any. If they would [have] been true we would have been in France [a] long time ago.

This is why the 34th Infantry became known as the "Sandstorm Division."

Every thing is the same here. We have another concert to morrow night. We played four allready this week.

They are going to show 6000 feet of moving pictures at our Y. Fri. Mon. + Tues. taken in camp here and then they will send the film north, so when it comes to St. Paul you want to take in that picture.

So Olga says shes been getting thin. Well its a good thing the goverment made a meatless day and wheatless days.[26] I am sure thats the only thing that made her a little thiner. So them days did some good didn't they? We got iron beds or cots this week. They are pretty nice. We sleep like logs now. They have pretty good springs in them too.

I have not heard from Standley, but I have wrote to him every once in awhile.

To bad your having such bad weather, it auto get warm pretty soon.

I saw Art Smith to day. Hes same as ever. Most of [the] svea boys are out to the range so they only come in six hours every sunday. Art H. is better two. Well news is scarce to night so I will close with Love to All

Marland

Write soon.

Tell Olga I am waiting for those pictures to see how thin she has gotten. If she is still pretty fat, I will write Pres. Wilson to put in more meatless days. don't you think so Pa. Ha. Ha

Marland's Lament: "Every thing is the same here"

Marland Williams, now Musician 2nd Class, frequently grouses, albeit gently, about the protracted training period at Camp Cody. Days in the camp's tent city and the monotonous barren high desert that surrounded it could drag. Sterile, unpainted wood-frame buildings held mess halls and recreational buildings that added to the sameness. On March 14, 1918, Marland wrote to his family, "Every thing is the same here." He did keep busy as a member of the 125th F. A. band, playing at military functions, funerals, concerts, churches and more. But he and his buddies had

---

26. With the slogan "Food Will Win the War," the U.S. Food Administration urged American families to do their part for the war effort by reducing consumption of key staples. More than 13 million families signed a pledge to observe "Meatless Monday" and "Wheatless Wednesday," http://www.meatlessmonday.com/about-us/history/.

signed up to fight, and yearned to get overseas and into the action.

As a bandsman, Marland understood camp routine better than many. The full band marched through Cody's tent streets daily at 5:30 a.m. blasting music at sleeping soldiers, rousing everyone. Reveille followed. Buglers sounded calls for the various activities as the day progressed. Camp Cody went quiet when Taps was sounded at 11. That process began anew the following day. Sunday was an exception—a day off, with the soldiers relatively free of duty.

Marland's March 14th letter shares rumors "about us moving" overseas, but then, in resignation, he adds, "But we hear so many stories. We don't believe any. If they [rumors] would have been true we would have been in France [a] long time ago." At the time Marland composed those comments, the 125th Field Artillery, 34th Division was entering its eighth month of training.

Four more months of Camp Cody life remained for the men who, living in tedium and beset by swirling desert winds, called themselves the "Sandstorm Division." The 125th F. A. finally moved out in July for Fort Sill, Oklahoma, where they underwent advanced training. By September, the troops reached Long Island, New York. And the World War was still an ocean away.

Sundays provided the only time off for men of the 125th F. A. Note the instrument case and bass drum.

125ᵀᴴ FIELD ARTILLERY BAND
CAMP CODY, NEW MEXICO

Mon. Mar 25 1918

Dear Sister + All

I suppose you are waiting for a letter. Time goes so fast and we are pretty busy so I kind of put if off. I am feeling fine, and dandy. The weather is getting pretty hot now.

We got our gass masks yesterday and we drill two hours a day with them now and we have to carry them with us all the time so we get good and used to them. We have to put them on in 6 seconds, so you see we cannot be very slow about it.

I have not heard from Standley yet. I hope Elen gets over her opperation all right.

[Marland's aunt Ellen (Peterson) Anderson, his father's younger sister]

Soldiers needed to train for the nightmare of poison gas attacks. Respirators similar to these were being used in France.

It sure takes a lot of music for our bands. They send $800 00 [$12,716] worth the other day and we have a few times that much all ready.

I hear they are going to show them movies of Camp Cody in St Paul soon. Say they are not like it is at all here. All the scenery is taken many miles from here. They only show the nice part of deming. They do not show no mexican houses or any thing like that. it allso shows fruit farms. Why they are many miles from here. The mines are from 40 to 65 miles from here you see these pictures were taken by an Iowa man so he shows mostly Iowa and Neb. boys. My the Minn boys were mad when they saw them pictures. Why the Minn boys got it over any Regiment in camp here 10 times. The same with our Art [artillery]. The pictures are good eles but its the best fake I ever saw of Deming. I will close now and write soon

Marland.

I am waiting for those pictures.

Deming, New Mexico, was organized in 1902. It was an entry point near the U.S.-Mexico border.

[Envelope with a three-cent stamp addressed to Miss Olga Williams, 391 Arundel St, St. Paul, Minn.]

125ᵀᴴ FIELD ARTILLERY BAND
CAMP CODY, NEW MEXICO

Mar 27 1918

Dear Sister + All.

I received your letter to day and was glad to hear you are all well. I also received a letter from Sidney and Aunty Emily. They told all the news at Svea.

I suppose you feel pretty big now [that you] got a new coat + hat + etc. How about little Jewel. She never says any thing about getting new things. Its a good thing I ain't there. Papa would not be able to keep up all of us. I got my fifth pair of shoes last week so its good they are free.

Say when they had target practise here I got hold of a 3 in Shell or bullet. I am sending one home by express for you to keep for me. I consider it a good relic. Its the same kind that Standleys out fit used to. Don't be fraid of it as there is nothing in it to go off. There is also a few lead bullets or shrapnell in it So I put some paper inside to keep them from rattling to much. So when you get

A soldier holds a 15-pound shell used in U.S. three-inch field guns.

this shell, screw the head off and take that paper off or out. This shell has been shot 4 ½ miles. Do not show this around to any out siders as it might cause trouble.

We had Regimental review to night. To morrow we have brigade review.

We finished our gass drills to day. Yesterday we were down and went throu the gass house where the gass was strong enough to kill a person if it were not for our mask. They made us take a breath of it and that was enough. We also had tear gass. you auto see the water run down our cheeks. Then they gave us gren cross gass[27] which works on the lungs and eyes. You auto seen some of the fel- lows when they got one little breath of that. Some fainted some threw up. But it gives us a good idea what gass is like and how neccesary masks are.

Well I will close now with love to all Marland.

A closer look at a gas mask shows the hose from the mask leading into an air-purifying respirator carried in a shoulder bag.

★ ★ ★

"WITH THE COLORS"
YMCA

Camp Cody
April 5 1918

Dear Sisters + All.

I will now answer your letter, which I recieved Thursday.

We have played a concert every night so We have been pretty busy. We allso had another division review to day. Last Thursday we

27. Marland refers to phosgene, a deadly chemical warfare agent employed by German troops during the Great War. German artillerists marked shells carrying the gas with a green cross to designate its purpose. Phosgene is a chemical that, above 47 degrees Fahrenheit, becomes a deadly gas. It attacks the lungs of those inhaling it. When concentrated and released phosgene appeared to soldiers as a fog-like cloud. Phosgene became the most deadly chemical used during the war. The Medical Department of the United States in the World War, Vol. 14, *Medical Aspects of Gas War*, provides a detailed review of "war gases," see http://www.gwpda.org/medical/gaswar/gas.htm. National Institute for Occupational Safety and Health, Classification and Methods of Use of War Gases, "Phosgene: Lung Damaging Agent," https://www.cdc.gov/niosh/ershdb/emergencyresponsecard_29750023.html.

played another funeral.

Say some of the fellows have been getting letters from St Paul saying that on the barns out at Fort Snelling there are signs (125 Field Artillery). Will you see if there is any thing too this or not. I have an idea we are going to leave here soon. It would be to good to get back to fort Snelling.

I suppose you are having nice weather. I bet Papa is figuring where he can plant some flowers.

I was over in Art. Smiths tent awhile to night. Hes feeling fine. He said every thing is fine in Bay City. I suppose you here Louy Andrew is dead. I wonder what they will do with Dewey. You auto see the dogs we have around here. The soldiers can do any thing with them, but they can't stand a civilian.

Dogs were "enlisted" as mascots at Camp Cody. Violet, pictured here, lived with Marland's unit.

Whats a matter with pa couldn't he find room to get on the picture. My mamma sure looked fine on those pictures and so did Jewel and you.

So you and Jewell are getting to be some singers thats good. and practise a lot. Well news is scarce to night, so I will close this time with love to all

Marland

★ ★ ★

"WITH THE COLORS"
YMCA

Camp Cody, N.M.
1918

Dear Sisters + All.

I will write you a few lines and let you know I received your box of good candy. Man thanks it sure was good.

I am feeling better than ever. The weather is swell now. But the nights get quiet cool.

I suppose you had a lot of eggs [at] easter. We each had two. So we had a reminder any how. One of the boys in my tent also got a box from home with a few eggs in it so we had another egg.

Tents and their contents at dusty Camp Cody get an airing.

I have not heard from Standley. Have you? If you havent, don't worry because if they are up near the front, they will hardly have any chance to write and if any thing should happen the government always notifies. So don't worry.

Seeing you have sent me so much, I hope you have sent Standley just as much. I would rather you send him than me. It is hard for him to get any thing over there. So if you send a few hankerchifs, towel, cigars and little things like that. Don't send much in a package as they might get lost and it wont amount to much. You can't hardly realize how nice it is to get something from home.

I suppose you are looking for that shell. Well I havent been down to the express office with it yet. I will try and send it this week. Well news is scarce so I will close With Love to All

Marland.

I am waiting to See those pictures yet.

Camp Cody
April 11 1918

Dear Father + All.

Will write you a few lines to night and let you know I am feeling fine.

Its been pretty warm out to day. We are working the same as ever. I was over [at] Batt, B. a little while to night. I heard that Ray Fauts [Fouts] is dead.[28] He used to be in L. Co. But trans-

---

28. Actually, Raymond Kennedy Fouts was not dead. He was born November 18, 1895, in Wisconsin, and died August 31, 1960, in Spokane, Washington, Ancestry.com, "*Washington, Deaths, 1883–1960.*"

ferred out in too the machine gun battlion when we went in too Artillery. I saw him about 3 week ago and he was looking fine than. Pneumonia is pretty hard on them here yet.

A couple of my fillings fell out and I need to have that fixed right away. But you see in the army all they are allowed to do is to fill them with cement or pull them. Now I dont think cement will hold so the denest down town will fix them for $10.00 [$159]. So I am going to have him do it. Now Olga said you put that first twenty dollars I sent home in the bank. Now if you will draw that and send me $10 so I can get my teeth fixed right away as the denst don't do credit work. you keep the other $15 [$238]. I am sure you can use them. You will need a suit I sup-

pose and that will help a little. I would pay for it out of my salary but you see, I only draw 9.60 [$153] and it takes that much for other stuff amonth. I am getting pretty close on money. I didnot spend any of my money to day and go to circus. I have not been to a show for a long time and I dont drink or smoke so you see I try and be care ful. I wont take any more bonds and as soon as I get those I have paid up I will be able to send a little money home. The little interest that $25 [$397] draws don't mount to much so its better you use it. Can I expect that $10 soon so I know arangment to make with the dentist.

Marland poses by a wash tub.

I see by the paper you cannot send over any more packages across the sea unless the party there asks for it. and then you can only send what he asks for. You had better look that rule up before you send Standley any more or he might not get it. I wish we would go soon. Well good night.

With Love to All,
Marland

One of the wood-frame mess halls used by soldiers of the 125th F. A.

Camp Cody
April 11 1918

Dear Sister + All.

I received papas letter Monday, Glad to hear you are all well. I am feeling better than ever.

We played a concert to night, and after that Art Smith and Art Olson [of Red Wing's Company L] walked with me over to the tent, They just left now.

Papa said I should write a long letter, but I dont know what to write about. I am in bed now writing so I have to use a pencil. I washed my clothes to day. I am quiet a wash women now. They have an electric iorn [iron] here, so we also press our pants and shirts.

I have not heard from Standley either. I have asked some of the boys here who have friends in the same Regiment and they have not heard either. So I think hes in a place where they cannot write. The government always notifies if one get injured so don't worry.

Christin does not get any of Petes insurance But even at that, It would not hurt is [if] she got a little of it. She did more for Pete than one realizes.

All the Svea boys are alright, I have not seen Chester for a few months. Hes not in our Regiment. I am goin to sleep now will finish in the morning.

I just finished breakfast now and as they collect mail in about 10 mineuts I will close With Love to all

Marland

★ ★ ★

Camp Cody N.M.
April 12, 1918

Dear Sisters And All.

I receive your letter to day. that little note was best of all. I sure am glad Standley is safe and that he has had a raise. You know I have always said you need not worry, because he always makes good. I suppose you think its time I make a showing. I might have a chance soon for a raise as the other baritone player went to the hospital to day. He is all run down and he might get a discharge. Hes been kind of sick all the time and is not very strong. We played a funeral to day. They sent Ray Fauts [Fouts] too Red Wing this after noon. He died in 8 days with pneumonia.

Band members chat while waiting for a funeral.

It rained a little to night so I its a little chilly, but we cut a little wood and got a fire, so we are comfortable. It sure was dusty before the rain but now its fresh and nice.

You seem to think I am getting to be quiet a player. Well I [am] learning a little every day. I don't mind if we stay in the army another year, althou I sure would like a visit home. I am pretty used to being away now. To morrow its 9 months since I left home. It does not seem so long.

So you say you quiet taking lessons because you are getting so thin. I must say you look a little thiner, but a few more lessons won't hurt you. I am glad Jewell has started. Let [her] practise my cornett too if she wants to. You will see that soon there will be many girl bands and it will be great for her. But it nice for her to play the piano too. You practise on the cornet too. It wont hurt your lips.

Well news is scarce so I will close for this time With Love to All
Marland
Write soon

★ ★ ★

Camp Cody. N.M.
April 16. 1918.

Dear Sisters + all.

I received Papas letter yesterday. I am feeling better than ever. I will only write a few words this morning but I thought I let you know I heard from Standley as you [are] anxious to know I will enclose his card. This card shows that he is now allowed to write letters.

Every thing is about the same here. Tell Papa I don't know any on that picture. Well its time for breakfast so I will have to go and eat. I will write more later.

Marland

Due to his last name of Williams, Marland was nicknamed "Bill" by his army buddies.

★ ★ ★

Camp Cody N. M.
April 20, 1918

Dear Sisters + All.

I received the money and the other letter O.K. Glad to hear you are all well. I am feeling fine, but one of the boys in our company got the mumps a couple days a go, so now we are quarnteened for 3 weeks. Some luck. We can't leave our street only on duty when we dont mix with other Batteries. Battery "B" is also quarnteened for mumps.[29]

Things look more like moving to day than ever. I think we are sure to leave here soon. We are going to have our over sea examination Monday. They Put them in three classes. "A" goes across, "B" stays here and "C" gets a discharge. I hope I get "a." I don't see why I shouldn't.

I will send Standleys letter back as you might want it. Its funny

29. Contagious diseases plagued American training bases. Loss of soldiers to death or disability was tragic for families involved, but also damaging to unit strength and morale. In April 1918, mumps, a viral disease causing fever, muscle ache and fatigue, struck Camp Cody. Outbreaks of measles and pneumonia also hit the camp in 1917 and early 1918.

he does not get any of my letters. I wrote him quiet often.

My its been cold here to day. The [nights] have been quiet cold too. We have four blankets and I put my over coat on top and I freeze sometimes anyhow.

The sand still blows and every thing else is about the same.

After supper a few of us fellows took our horns and went out in our street and played a few pieces. It sure cheers the bunch up. You don't relize what music does in a place like this. Well I will close this time With love to all

Marland.

Marland, second from left, stands with members of the 125th F. A. jazz band. The drum is from their former Minnesota National Guard unit.

Camp Cody's saxophone group

Camp Cody NM
April 30. 1918

Dear Sisters + All.

Will answer your letter I received to day. and also let you know I am feeling fine.

Just think its a year ago to day since I enlisted. Only a week after Standley, and he's been in France so many months and I am here yet. I think they are afraid of Mexican trouble and they are holding us for border protection. don't say anything around about this. You see we can see Mexico from camp here, and villin [village] is not very far off.[30]

The "business end" of a U.S. three-inch gun

The other day they had a sort of sham battle here. They fixed up three emaginary enemy trenches and block house and then our soldiers placed their cannons around 3 ½ or 4 miles away and also many machine guns. They started firing at these then. We were on a hill between the trenches and the guns watching the shells explod on the trenches. It sure was some noise. Just like sharp thunder. we could here the bullets whisling over our heads all the time. we got a good idea what we have to go throu over there.

Say did you get that shell I sent you. Let me know if you did.

I washed my clothes after supper to night. I am quiet a wash woman now. To morrow we start to wear our cotton uniforms and underwear. It is not very warm here let [yet] and the nights are

A motorized trench digger used at Camp Cody

quiet chilly. my but the sands have been blowing these last few days. You sure are patriotic. Glad to see it. With Love to All

Marland

Write soon

30. The Mexico-U.S. border had been tense since the beginning of the Mexican Revolution in 1910. Forces of both nations fought occasionally. A 1916 cross-border raid into Columbus, New Mexico—the future Camp Cody was 25 miles north of Columbus—by a Mexican revolutionary unit prompted a strong U.S. response. Gen. John J. Pershing, the man who would lead U.S. troops in the World War, took some 14,000 American soldiers into Mexico. The border region remained tense through 1919. Red Wing's Minnesota National Guard Company L, part of Pershing's 1916 army, returned to New Mexico a year later to prepare for the war in Europe.

★ ★ ★

Camp Cody NM
May 7. 1918

Dear Father Mother + all.

I will try and write you a few lines to night and let you know I am feeling fine. We have been so busy that I dont have no spare time at all. This week we have been playing all most all the time. Sunday we played three concerts. last night [a] dance, to night one and to night a concert besides our regular work, which now is much more than usual. I hear we are going to have an all day hike to morrow. Besides its so hot now. I think it passed the 100 mark. But just the same I am feeling better than ever and as comfortable as can be.

I had a letter from Standley Fri. written April 11. He was feeling fine. No extra news what ever. I hope I will be near him soon. I also had a letter from Sidney. He said John Mackuster is dead. Also that Uncle Edd has moved on Samulsons place now. Sidney is the only one in the relation that thinks I am good enough to write too I guess. Emelie always put in a few nice words to.

I bet Olga will be glad when the twelfth is over.[31] Say papa you told me to look that up Well I can not get down town for sometime so I am sorry I wont to be able to get that. I will remember that a little later.

I bet you feel pretty good now that you have the farm settled and also a little jack [left] over. That was a good surprise to me. I never knew you had that R.W. [Red Wing] house till now.[32] My the girls are sure working hard for the Red Cross. But it's good work and every cent is put to some good use. Well I will close now with love to all

Marland
Write soon.
I also made Class A. O.K. [passed the physical for overseas duty] say did you get that shell.

31. Olga was confirmed on May 12, 1918, at First Lutheran Church in St. Paul, Minnesota.
32. In October 1917, Alvin bought a house on Red Wing's Sturtevant St. for $2,000 [$41,250]. His family never lived there and he sold it six months later for $1,800 [$28,610]. It is not known if he planned to live there or if he made the purchase as an investment.

★ ★ ★

Camp Cody N.M.
May 16 1918

Dear Father + All.

Will answer your letter, which I received to day. It is 11 oclock now, and I am in bed, but you see we are going on a 7 or 8 day hike and might not have a chance to write till we come back. I have been working steady since 6 oclock this morning so I am a little tired. We all have horses to ride. I got a dandy one like Syrus. I just finished fixing up my saddle equipment. We have an awfull lot of things to carry with us. We had a regular wild west ride yesterday. we rode 15 miles throu the prairie over ditches and cactus on a gallop allmost all the way. Its sure fun. Two of the fellows got bucked off.

I suppose Olga is happy now. The weather is fine here now. The svea boys are all well. Albins [Gustafson] address is Batt. B. 125 F.A. I saw Art Smith to day. He's the same as ever. Well I will quite now as we have to get up 5 oclock and get ready.

With Love to All
Marland

A column of soldiers from the 125th F. A. takes part in desert maneuvers. A few men take a break, while Marland's horse, "Number 87," poses for a photo.

★ ★ ★

125ᵀᴴ FIELD ARTILLERY BAND
CAMP CODY, NEW MEXICO

May 26-18

Dear Sister + all

I will answer your welcome letter I received to day. I also got the box to day. Tell mamma the cake sure was find and many thanks.

We just got back this morning on [a] 7 day hike. I sure had a dandy time. I had my own horse I did some wild west riding too. I was with scouts some and then I was messenger for the commader of the second battalion. When he sent a message we had to ride over mountians, ditches and brush as fast as our horses could gallop. Some fun. We were having battles all the time. some racket when them cannons are shooting. we went to Ft Cuming an old Indian Fort.[33] Some place. Its all in ruins now right below the foot of mount cook. one of the highest mountains in new Mex. Our worst trouble was to get water.

Lunchtime in the field

We sure were dirty when we got back as it was awful dusty. Last night they got us up 12 oclock and we were in camp here before breakfast, riding 20 miles in the dark. We had some feed on our trip too. We had boiled bacon, cold tomatoes Hard tack and black coffee. We got beans 3 times and potatoes twice. How would Pa like to live on that for a week and ride all day in the saddle.

I bet you are glad you are confirmed now.

Oil-spraying trucks, like the one shown here, helped control dust on camp roads.

33. Fort Cummings was established in 1863 at the site of Cooke's Spring in present-day Luna County, New Mexico, northwest of the future Camp Cody site. It provided protection to travelers from the hostile Chiricahua Apaches fighting against American incursions into Apache territory. The military abandoned the fort in 1873, but returned in the mid-1880s when the Apache wars continued. "The Wrath of Cochise," in *Through Indian Eyes, The Untold Stories of Native American People* (New York: Reader's Digest Assn., 1995) 304-305. http://www.legendsofamerica.com/nm-fortcummings.html.

Our director has had no programs latley, so could not send any. They hauled our instruments on the hike so we played a concert almost every night.

I don't think we can go to Duluth as we can not get off. I wish they would move us over soon. The sand is just a bad as ever.

Well news is scarce so will close as I want to goto bed.

With Love to all

Marland

Write soon.

ask mamma if I have any cotton socks left if she would please send them. We cannot hardy get any socks here.

Camp Cody N.M.
May 29. 1918.

Dear Sister + All.

I received your picture to day and sure was glad to get it. It sure is a dandy. I was realy surprised. and I must admit your getting thinner. Are you going to send Pearly [Wiberg of Trenton] one?

I am feeling fine and every thing is the same. We had an awfull sand storm to day, but we are so used to them now. I bet Mamma would go wild if you would have a sand storm like that and get the house full of sand.

I have not heard from Standley yet, but don't worry for hes safe only under conditions where he cant write. I only wish I enlisted with him. But maybe I am better off here. So long as one wears the uniform he does all he can. The drafted birds are still coming in by the train loads. Papa can feel Proud that Standley was not drafted. We all had to hand in a blanket to day so they (the draft) would have some to sleep with. They also gave us new coats so we could give them our old ones.

I suppose school is soon out. But I suppose you feel much better that confirmation is over and you can rest your mind a little.

Well good night and many thanks for the picture It sure was a dandy and Love to All

Kid.

★ ★ ★

HEADQUARTERS COMPANY 125TH FIELD ARTILLERY
"WITH THE COLORS" WHEREVER THEY GO

Camp Cody N.M.
June 9. 1918

Dear Folks.

I received Papas letter this morning and glad to hear you [are] all well. I feel better than ever my self. The weather has been pretty hot here now, but we have had a few showers to settle the sand a little. So that helps some.

Every thing is about the same here. The same thing over day after day. Glad to hear Standley is well. I only wish I were with him. I think I can stand it about as well. But may be I am better off But a fellows hates to be down here where nothing can be done. But I can fell good I am in an organisation that does as much good as any and that is the band. You Auto see the boys when we play for them. Even if they are tired after their days work. They brighten

The 125th Field Artillery band rehearsing outdoors

right up. on the march they pick right up as soon as they hear the music. It would be great if they would send our band over and play to the fellows there. I will enclose a clipping and you can see your self.

I have ordered that horn [double-bell euphonium] through are leader from C.G. Conn. He can get all dicounts there as he has handled their instruments. He knows them well and is more apt to get a better instrument for the money.

You asked if I felt older No I do not. [Marland's 19th birthday was June 5th.] I feel like the same kid. And I believe I would be as bad as [I] used to if I were home. It would be fun to chew the Rag again, wouldnt it Dad. Well will close this time with love to all

Marland

Double-Bell Euphonium

The only knowledge that many people have of the double-bell euphonium is from Meredith Willson's song "Seventy-six Trombones" in his 1957 Broadway musical and the 1962 movie *The Music Man*:

Seventy-six trombones caught the morning sun, with a hundred and ten cornets right behind.

There were more than a thousand reeds springing up like weeds,

There were horns of every shape and kind.

There were copper-bottomed timpani in horse platoons, thundering, thundering, all along the way.

Double-bell euphoniums and big bassoons…[34]

His double-bell euphonium stayed with Marland through the war years and for the rest of his life.

A euphonium is the tenor voice of the tuba family. Typically it has one bell and four valves, but around 1880 a double-bell version was introduced, which remained popular in American bands until about 1930. It was the standout instrument of any music ensemble. On these duplex horns, a fifth valve routes the player's air to one bell or the other. This instrument has a conical bore, which produces a rich, mellow quality from the larger bell. The smaller bell produces a brighter, thinner sound.

Depending on the music, players used the large bell to blend with the tubas, and the smaller bell to blend with the trombones. Soloists also switched between bells to produce an echo effect. A mute placed in the smaller bell accentuated the echo and different tone quality.

The instrument began to disappear from manufacturers' catalogs in the 1930s. The reasons may have been the cost of manufacturing the horn and the inconsistent tuning between the two bells. Another factor may have been the introduction of the British euphonium with a larger bore, which produced a darker and mellower tone. By the 1950s the British-style horn was the preferred instrument and composers ceased writing parts for the double-belled euphonium.

Marland was justifiably proud of his new horn. He continued to play this instrument throughout his adult life with the Cannon Falls City Band—occasionally as a soloist.

Now the double-bell euphonium is regarded as a novelty, popular with certain performers, collectors, and those seeking a curious wall ornament for their music rooms or drinking establishment. Marland's horn is in the possession of his granddaughter—also a musician—and will remain a family heirloom.

34. Meredith Willson, *The Music Man*, (New York: Frank Music, 1957).

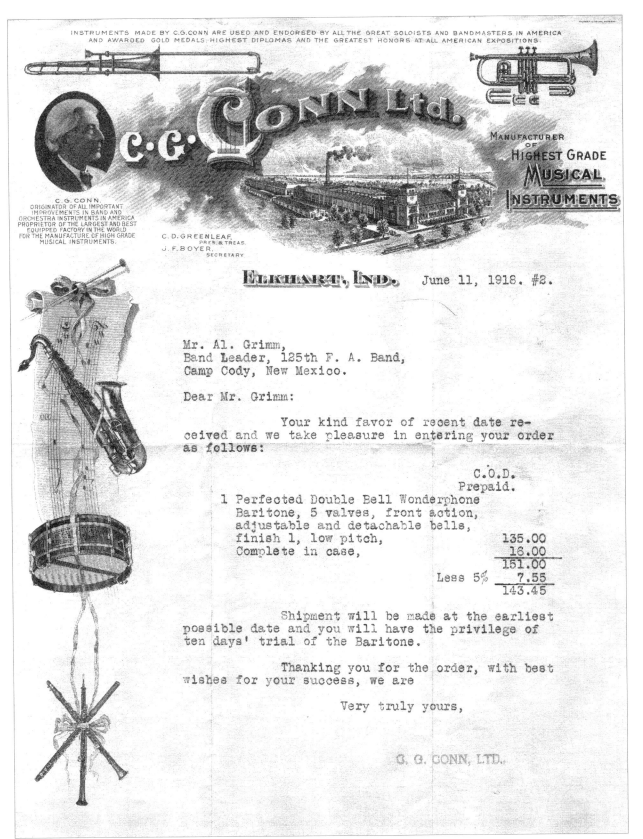

INSTRUMENTS MADE BY C.G.CONN ARE USED AND ENDORSED BY ALL THE GREAT SOLOISTS AND BANDMASTERS IN AMERICA AND AWARDED GOLD MEDALS, HIGHEST DIPLOMAS AND THE GREATEST HONORS AT ALL AMERICAN EXPOSITIONS.

C. G. CONN Ltd.

MANUFACTURER OF HIGHEST GRADE MUSICAL INSTRUMENTS

C. G. CONN.
ORIGINATOR OF ALL IMPORTANT IMPROVEMENTS IN BAND AND ORCHESTRA INSTRUMENTS IN AMERICA PROPRIETOR OF THE LARGEST AND BEST EQUIPPED FACTORY IN THE WORLD FOR THE MANUFACTURE OF HIGH GRADE MUSICAL INSTRUMENTS.

C. D. GREENLEAF,
PRES. & TREAS.
J. F. BOYER,
SECRETARY

ELKHART, IND.   June 11, 1918. #2.

Mr. Al. Grimm,
Band Leader, 125th F. A. Band,
Camp Cody, New Mexico.

Dear Mr. Grimm:

　　　　　Your kind favor of recent date received and we take pleasure in entering your order as follows:

```
                                        C.O.D.
                                        Prepaid.
   1 Perfected Double Bell Wonderphone
      Baritone, 5 valves, front action,
      adjustable and detachable bells,
      finish 1, low pitch,                135.00
      Complete in case,                    16.00
                                          151.00
                           Less 5%          7.55
                                          143.45
```

　　　　　Shipment will be made at the earliest possible date and you will have the privilege of ten days' trial of the Baritone.

　　　　　Thanking you for the order, with best wishes for your success, we are

　　　　　　　　　Very truly yours,

　　　　　　　　　　　　　　　C. G. CONN, LTD.

Marland's bill for the double-bell euphonium. His letters show how determined he was to acquire the instrument.

[Envelope with a three-cent stamp addressed to Mr. Alvin Williams, 391 Arundel St, St. Paul, Minn.]

HEADQUARTERS COMPANY 125ᵗʰ FIELD ARTILLERY
"WITH THE COLORS" WHEREVER THEY GO

Camp Cody N.M.
June 18 1918

Dear Father + All.

I received Olgas letter to day. Glad to hear you are all well. I am feeling fine as usual. The weather sure is hot. We had a little shower last night.

I suppose you were rather surprised to get that telegram. Well the horn came quicker than I expected, and the officers and band leaders tried to get the horn out of the express office but could not till the money was deposited. and they will hold the money till the trial is up on the horn and if I except the horn they will send the money to Conn and if I do not take it all the money will be refunded so we will not be out any. I am practicing all I can now, so you can depend up on me doing my best.

Last Sunday we played for church then we went up to the base hospital and gave a concert. After dinner we marched 360 boys from our Regiment to the train. They are bound for France. Quite a few Red Wing boys were in the bunch. After that we went over and played for a ball game. Last night we played a dance. So you see we are keep busy. I have an Idea we are going to move to another camp soon. I hope so at least.

There are over six thousand more draft[ees] coming here next week.[35]

I suppose you are having some

Camp Cody soldiers watch a baseball game.

35. Marland and other early arrivals at Camp Cody volunteered for National Guard service and were then "federalized" into the U.S. Regular Army. In May 1917, Congress ordered a national draft of men to meet wartime needs. Thousands of draftees began arriving at Camp Cody as the training of Sandstorm Division neared an end. Selective Service Systems, "Induction Statictics [sic]" reports that 516,212 men were drafted into military service in 1917; some 2.3 million were inducted in 1918. https://www.sss.gov/About/History-And-Records/Induction-Statistics; Mark Sullivan, *Our Times: America at the Birth of the Twentieth Century* [condensed version, Dan Rather, editor] (New York: Scribner, 1996) 518–521.

hot weather to now. It must be hard for you to be still when you have no garden to putter around in.

I have not heard from Standley either. But don't worry. He will take care of himself. I only wish we were to gather.

Well news is scarce so will close with Love to all

Marland

P.S. I suppose you think that a very dear price for my horn, but that is wholesale with an extra 5% discount so you see I am getting some horn.[36] It will be the best one in camp.

HEADQUARTERS COMPANY 125TH FIELD ARTILLERY "WITH THE COLORS" WHEREVER THEY GO

Camp Cody
June 20 1918

Dear Father.

Will write you a few lines to night and let you know I am feeling well

I will enclose the bill to the horn so you can see the prize [price]. You see they sent it C.O.D. 10 day trial, but in order to get it out of the express company. I have to deposit full amount and they hold the money till trial is over, and if I except the horn they will pay Conn the money and if the horn is not satisfactory I get the money back and they send the horn back.

So that's why I sent you a night telegram Tuesday for you to wire me the money and now it is Thursday night and I have recived no answer from you. Did you not get the telegram. now they only hold express six days here so they will send it back Saturday if I don't deposit the money. Now in order for me to get the horn out one of the boys here said he will pay for it tomorow and I will pay him as soon as you send me the money. I know its a high prize for a horn, but its a dandy, and you said I should get a good one and you would send me the money when I get it. So I hope you will send it right

36. Marland's 1918 Conn Wonderphone double-bell euphonium cost $143.45 [$2,280]. This instrument is now in the possession of his granddaughter, Elizabeth Williams Gomoll.

away so I can pay that other fellow back. You know you will get my $200⁰⁰ [$3,178] Liberty bonds in Agust to pay for it. Now answer me on this letter so I know you understand and I hope every thing is satisfactory with you.

Love to all
Marland

HEADQUARTERS COMPANY 125ᵀᴴ FIELD ARTILLERY "WITH THE COLORS" WHEREVER THEY GO

Camp Cody N.M
June 24 1918

Dear Jewel and All.

I just received your letter, and glad to here you are all well. I am feeling better than ever. I think we are going to leave this camp in a coupl weeks maybe sooner. Its getting awful hot here now. I suppose its the same up there.

I like my new horn fine, but you tell papa if he dont send me the money right away I will have to send the horn right back. You see I have had it 7 days now and I can only keep it 10. I am getting kind of worried now be cause he don't send the money. I sent him a telegram and tow [two] letters now asking for it and he dont ever say nothing about it. He told me he would send me the money as soon as I asked for it. If he don't want to send me it. I wish he say so. The bill is $144.⁰⁰ [$2,289] But the horn is worth it. I hope this is the last time I will have to ask for money. I cant get my Liberty bonds till the Last of August or else I could have sold them and got the money. You know I promised him the bonds in return so he wont be any thing out.

I suppose you will be some player when I get home. Well practise hard now. We got a big concert to play up town to night. I wish you could hear us once.

I hope you have a good time down in svea. Well news is scarce so will close with Love to all
Marland.

★ ★ ★

[Envelope with a three-cent stamp addressed to Mr. Alvin Williams, 391 Arundel St, St. Paul, Minn.]

"WITH THE COLORS"
YMCA

Camp Cody N.M.
June 29 1918

Dear Dad and All

I will answer your letter I received yesterday now before I go to bed. I am feeling better than ever. We have every thing packed up now so we can leave in a couple hours notice. It looks as oh we might leave Tuesday maybe sooner and we dont even know where we are going. But it makes us feel good to know we our on our way.

I just received that money to night, "Many thanks." The telegram had got delayed 9 days on the road. I didnot know hardly what to do. I knew you would send the money as soon as you got word. but I feel good now it is straighten out. I have the nicest and best horn in camp now. We thought maybe we would have left this week, but I guess they held off a little on account of the new men we got.

I had a letter from Standley yesterday, also a picture of him self and another sergent on horse back. I thought maybe he sent you one too. but if he did not say so and I Will send mine home. He sure looks swell on it. He had no news atall.

I have a bunch of pictures I am going to send you maybe to day. Please take care of these till I get back. Let me know if you get them.

Troop trains like this one carried the 125th F. A. on long trips from Minnesota to New Mexico and later to Long Island, New York.

Well this is Sunday morning now. The wind is blowing to beat the band. We have to go down and play church for the drafted men a 7.30 and then come back and play for our Regiment. We might play a concert at the Hospital too so we will be kind of busy.

Marland waited for a gradual curve to take this photo of his troop train.

We got orders this morning to load all our things on the train to day.

Albin Gustafson has had operation for pendicitus. If he has not told his folks what it was, maybe you had better now

not] say any thing to them. He is doing fine.

Well I will have to get busy now so will closs. We get up 5,15 now so we are kind of early birds. Many thanks for the money. I have every thing settled now.

With Love to All
Marland

[Postcard with two one-cent stamps addressed to Mr. Alvin Williams, 391 Arundel St., St. Paul, Minn.; upper left corner: Distributed by the Canteen Service of The American Red Cross.]

July 2, 1918
Dear Folks.
    Just arrived in Elpaso. We have been traveling right on the mexican border all the time. El Paso is sure a pretty place. We do not know where we are going. We are right by the Reo Grande River now.
Marland

"WITH THE COLORS"
YMCA

Fort Sill. Okla.
July 5 1918

Dear Folks.

Will drop you a line and let you know where I am. We came here to Fort Sill yesterday morning.[37] This is a heaven [compared] to where we came from. We all like it fine.

This camp is much larger, only artillery and aviation here. The[re] is a bunch a Machines in the air all the time here.

I only have a mineut to write so will close.

Marland

Will write more soon

★ ★ ★

"WITH THE COLORS"
YMCA

Fort Sill Okla.
July 10 1918

Dear Sister and All.

Have been waiting for a letter but as I have not received any thought I had better write any way. I am feeling fine and hope you are all the same.

This camp sure is a nice place. I only wish we could have been here all the time instead [of] Cody. The weather is pretty hot here. Night before yesterday we had a hard electric storm. They are

37. In 1917 the War Department ordered the reopening of the School of Fire for Field Artillery at Fort Sill, Oklahoma, after combat preparations in division camps, according to one study, "proved to be completely inadequate at training the field artillery units." Jonathan T. Palumbo, "*U.S. Field Artillery after World War I: Modernizing the Force While Downsizing*," Master of Military Art and Science Theses, Command and General Staff College, June 13, 2014, 34–38, quote 37.

drilling the fellows pretty hard here as we expect to leave for France the Last of August. I hope I can see Standley when we get over. We have played a concert here almost every day or night.

There sure is some noise around here all day long as they are shoot cannons, machine guns, rifles, and revolvers all the time Then there is that noise from the areoplanes.[38] There are 10 or 15 in the air all the time. I saw one fall saturday and the driver got killed.

The planes Marland writes about are likely Curtis JN-4s, the famed "Jenny." This Jenny is landing at Fort Sill.

They also have them big observation balloons here to. There are quiet a number of Regulars here. They live in big barracks. They or some of them have been here 4 or 5 years.

I was down to see Clarance Kask a couple days ago but he went home the day before on a furlough fore Gramma Kasks funeral.[39] You might see him in St Paul. I had a letter from Sidney Wensday.

We live in tents here the same as Cody. The[y] put in the wires for electric lights to day. So we will have it pretty nice now. We got a bunch of new clothes to day. I got 1 shirt 1 pair pants, 2 suits cotton underwear 1 hat 1 pair socks 1 pair leggans, so I am pretty well fitted out.

We have not got our horses any more now. We got a bunch of moter trucks to do our hauling now.

Say Olga that last letter I wrote about that money looks as oh you misunderstood it, because in your last letter you wrote as oh I thought papa would not give me that money, but that was not the case. I knew when papa said he would give it I knew he would. But you see, I knew we were going to move and we were not allowed

38. These airplanes were probably Curtis JN-4s, known as "Jennies." The Jenny was a well-constructed biplane with a dependable engine, but it was somewhat difficult to land. Pilots jokingly said this factor made it a good trainer, because "If you can fly a Jenny, you can fly anything!" By the end of the war, Curtiss and other companies had manufactured more than 5,500 JN-4s under government contract. http://www.glennhcurtissmuseum.org/the-jenny.php. For a film on the training of U.S. pilots for the World War see "WW1: Aviation Training in the United States," https://www.youtube.com/watch?v=Qwv4DEuW48c.

39. Clarence William Kask was born May 3, 1894, and died November 25, 1971. He served in Company I of the 351st Infantry during World War I. Clarence was related to Marland through Marland's aunt Olive, who married Charley Kask; Charley's brother Albert was the father of Clarence. "Grandma Kask" was Christine who lived with her son Albert and grandson Clarence in Trenton.

to say so, and as the money got delayed I thought I might not get it before we left cody. Thats why I wanted it in such a hurry. I hope you will understand now. Your letter made me feel kind a bad about it. So will close this time with Love to All

    Marland

    Write soon

[Envelope with three one-cent stamps addressed to Mr. Alvin Williams, 391 Arundel St, St. Paul, Minn.]

"WITH THE COLORS"
YMCA

Fort Sill Okla
July 18 1918

Dear Dad + Folks

    Will answer Olgas letter I received a couple days ago. I am feeling fine and like it better here right along. We just got throu playing a concert about 20 mineuts ago for the colonel. The weather is pretty hot here, not so bad as cody, but the nights are warmer.

    The boys are drilling pretty hard now. Albin, and Harold Sharp came up here this week Albin got over his operation fine. Harold is back in the company now. I suppose you know he was in the hospital since last October. He has an awful big cut back of his ear where he was operated on. Have you heard from Standley lately. You did not say whether you got a picture from him or not. If you did not say so and I will send you mine.

    Say Dad do you want any Cactus if so say so and I will send some home. There are quiet a few here in the hills. There is hardly anything to write about

Marland offered to send cactus home to his father, writing, "there are quite a few in the hills [around Fort Sill]."

as we have the same thing over day after day. and every thing is about the same. They are very few Svea boys left here now. Albert

Filn [possibly Albert Flynn, a Company L enlistee in 1917] is a bugler now, a dandy too. I saw A Smith and Gotfred last night they are same as always.

　　With Love to all
　　Marland.

★ ★ ★

"WITH THE COLORS"
YMCA

Fort Sill Okla
July 28 1918

Dear Dad + All.

Will write a few lines in answer to your letter. I am feeling better than ever and glad to hear you are all well. We just got throu with a concert a little while a go so its almost bed time now. We play a concert every night now except Sunday, when we play one in the forenoon. Every thing is about the same. I am sorry that I caused you so much extra trouble about that money. When you go in there you auto ball them out because they delayed it 10 days some wheres. Hows Hinckley Hope you had a good time.[40]

Clothes washing at hot and dusty Fort Sill

I have not heard from Standly either. The lights go out in a couple mineuts so will have to cut this short and get to bed. I washed my clothes to day, so have had no extra time at. all. the dust here is awfull dirty. Its pretty hot now and there are quiet a few flies. but it beats cody. Well good night to all

　　Kid

40. The family probably visited Alvin's sister, Ellen (Peterson) Anderson, who lived in Hinckley, Minnesota.

★ ★ ★

"WITH THE COLORS"
YMCA

Fort Sill Okla
July 29 1918

Dear Sister + All

I will answer your letter, which I received yester day. Glad to hear you are all well. I am feeling fine too. We just got throu playing for the colonel. I will enclose a week ago Saturday nights program. I was going to send it before but I forgot it. We dont very often get programs now.

I was out swimming at Medicine Park yesterday.[41] A truck from our company took us out. Its a summer resort. Its pretty nice to get away from camp once in awhile.

You said something about eats. Well I will down anything you send so if you make an extra cake or cookies, I would sure like one. But I [know] sugar is hard to get so that why I have not asked for any. One of the St, Paul boys in my tent got a big box saturday for his birthday, and you know what one fellow has in a tent is every bodys. so we had a swell feed. The army seems kind of funny

Taking a watermelon break, Marland on the left

because every[one] in their company are like brothers. They are all the time chewing the rag and play tricks on each other, but no body ever gets mad.

I guess they will fell [fill] our Regement up this week with drilled men from Waco Teaxas and it sounds as oh we might leave in side of a month. I hope so because this will be a sore bunch if we can't get accross after all the drilling we have did. We are drilled up good now to. You see we are six inch guns now instead of the 3 inch and

41. Medicine Park is a town near Lawton, Oklahoma, and has a long history as a cobblestone resort town. The cool water of Medicine Creek runs through a granite valley to the swimming hole at the center of town. This provided respite from hot summer weather for tourists and soldiers from nearby Fort Sill.

we have tractors to pull the guns.[42]

Well news is scarce so will close. I will enclose some pictures I want you to past in "the albin" for me. If you have any new ones you and the folks have taken send them down and I will sent them right back.

With Love Marland

Seeing you are doing so much for the Red Cross, would you do a little for me. I was wondering if you would make a cover or thing to put soap, tooth brush, razor and tolet articles in.

"WITH THE COLORS"
YMCA

Fort Sill Okla
Aug 5 1918

Dear Dad and all.

I suppose you think I am slow in answering, I don't mean to be, but we are so awful busy we don't have no time all [at] all. We just got thru with a concert at the Y.M.C.A. now.

I am feeling find and every thing is about the same. They make us work almost day and night now, and Sunday also. It looks as oh we will leave around the 18th or 20th. we are [to] get our clothes and equiment in shape for over seas now. We have only what clothes we need to get accross with now so we wont have much to carrey. We will have to send all our personal [belongings] home this week or 1st of next so I will have a few things to send home. any little thing I send home I hope you will keep for me. It might not look like much, but its some soveiner of places I have been.

You talk about moving on a farm again. I think you are really better off where you are. If you have money enough I would suggest you and Mamma buy a nice little 3, 4, or 5 room bungalow or house and

---

42. U.S. artillery units faced a dangerous shortage of field guns when America entered the war. In all, they had only 450 light field guns and 150 heavy cannon. The situation improved when they were supplied modern weapons by their French and English allies. Palumbo, "U.S. Field Artillery after World War I," 40–42. Thomas Fleming, *The Illusion of Victory* (New York: Basic Books, 2003) 103.

try and take it a little easy. Don't work to hard in the store. Maybe it would pay you to hire a little fellow to help around the store some. He could help dilever. Its to bad I can't be home to help. Now you know what I said here is my own thoughts about it. But you do as you like you know whats best. Then I was thinging this way. It won't be so long till Standley and I get back and I am sure we will get jobs in St Paul, and also stay at home. We might as well give our money to you and mamma as to pay board and room some other place. Say I have not got my bonds yet They are paid for and are signed to you. So the government auto send them to you soon. We have not been payed since in June and I hear we wont get paid till a couple days before we leave so that we will have some money when we go across.

Our Regiment has the highest mark in this camp, how is that. I see the 151 are sopposed to be the crack Regiment in France. I might see Standley be fore long. That sure would be nice to meet him there. But there is some talk we might go to Italy.

I saw Clarence Kask the other day. He is looking pretty good, as he just had a operation for appendicitus. He is married now. One of the boys in my tent got married last Saturday. His wife was out here all after noon She is from Duluth and a Swede too. A dandy little girl too. One of the boys in the next tent had his wife come a long with her and they have a house up a [at] Lawton. They are going to give us boys in the band a party Saturday night.

I suppose the girls are back from Hinckley now. Well its time for bed now so will close with Love to all. Good night.

Marland.

"WITH THE COLORS"
YMCA

Fort Sill Okla
Aug 11 1918

Dear Sister and all.

Will answer your letter which I received Friday. Glad you are all well. Did Standley say much in his last letter I think I will be near him in a month or so. There is some talk of we might go to Serbia. If we do we will go to the Pacific Coast, thru Japan across Russia and down thru Serbia [most likely Siberia]. It would take us between some 20 or 3[0] days on the water. That would be some trek tho wouldnt it. I do not know how true it is so don't say nothing out about it. Our officer also said he is sure of us leaving this month. We are working as hard as ever too. Last night we play a dance for the officers till 12.15. To night we play at the Aviation Field. I saw another aviator fall last week. He did not get hurt but he smashed his machine.

I was down to Lawton last week and had about another $10^{00} [$159] done on my teeth. I have only one poor tooth Left now, but I dont want to fix that till I get out of the army. as I want it crowned, and you see I might nock it out with my horn and when we are in camps far from a town I would not be able to get it set again and I would not be able to play.

That box you sent me sure was fine. The cake sure was swell. It will sure be fine to come home and get some good meals again. But I can't kick here we have all we wan't. The water is not very good here, but then we take ice out of the empty ice cream barrels and put in a pail so we get ice water. You see the band is nex to the canteen, so we get all the ice. That cover sure was dandy to. when I get my things in it, it fits just right in my pack bag.

I am sending another box of junk home. They wont let us take no personal things along so I thought it best to send them home. I put my Kodak in too and Olga you can have it. [This ended Marland's photographic record of the 125th F.A.] Have some one there sure [show] you how to you it. Its simple to run. It uses no [number] 120 film. get the Eastman they are the best. They cost 20¢ and you can take six pictures on a roll.

Soldiers were not allowed to bring personal items to Europe, thus ending Marland's photographic record.

Now take a picture of you bunch as Its over a year since I lift, so its quiet a while since [I] saw them. Besure and get Papa in as you left him out before. I know there was not room when you were in it, but you said you are thiner now so there might be room now. Well I dont know nothing more to write about so will close with Love to all

Marland

UNCLE WHO?

When you're confined to quarters
And you are layin' in your tent,
And you've got a canteen headache,
And your last two bits is spent,
And you're homesick for your mother,
And nobody gives a damn,
Then you're working for your Uncle,
Uncle who?---why Uncle Sam.

When you wake up in the mornings
And the flies buzz in your tent,
And you sort of start to wonder,
How your wife will pay the rent,
And the doctor has your number
So you can't pull any sham,
Then you're working for your Uncle,
Uncle who?---why Uncle Sam.

When they slam you in the guard house
'Cause you wouldn't shovel dirt,
And your heart is sort of aching,
And your feet are tired and hurt,
And you're waiting for court martial
Feelin' glum as any clam,
Then you're working for your Uncle,
Uncle who?--why Uncle Sam.

For you can't fool round your Uncle,
He's a sort of ornery gent.
Where you used to make a dollar,
Now he pays you 'bout a cent.
Just obey each little order
And don't growl about the chow,
For you're down here on the border
And you're in the army now.

---William Harvey Allen.

Unmailed postcard in Marland's album

"WITH THE COLORS"
YMCA

Fort Sill Okla
aug 21 1918

Dear Sister + All.

Will answer your letter now as it is a few mineuts before bedtime. We played a concert in the Regiment to night and on the way back I stopped at Art Smiths tent so its kind of late now. Art is the same as ever.

Its awful hot now, Way over a hundred every day. Some body is monking with the lights so I will have to stop now.

Well the lights are on again now. Say send that Standleys letter here to me, may be I can make it out. Dont show it to any one up there as they might say something out about it because if officers get ahold of it, they might go after Standley. They are awful strict about such things. So when you write to him, don't mention it.

We are getting more ready every day to leave. To day we got a Gilette safty razor, comb, shaving brush, and two towels. We have a big bunch of new men in the contact camp for quarteen so that will delay us some so I don't think we can leave till towards the 15tth now.

Have you took any pictures yet maybe I auto tell you how to use it. On clear days, have that little handel set on fifty. on cloudy on 25. Always have your back towards the sun or a little side ways don't hurt. Then there is another little lever for different views. Have it set on average view or when you get on how you can use your own judgement. When you take a roll down to get developed take only one print of each, then you can tell if they are good you can get more afterwards.

The government always notifies you in case we get hurt or any thing happens, but don't worry over that. We never thing of such a thing our selves.

I wash my cloths to day so you see there is always something extra to do. Well its bed time so will close with Love to All

Marland

★ ★ ★

"WITH THE COLORS"
YMCA

Fort Sill Okla
Aug 25–1918

Dear Sister and All.

I recieved your letter letter just be fore supper and I am down at the YMCA so I thought I would answer. We played our concert early to night–5,45-6,45 while the officers had supper. When we got thru they gave us some watermelon Then we went over and had our supper. So we are the free the rest of to night. They are going to have movies here to night.

Maybe you remembered me saying in another letter about the big observation balloons they had here. Well this after noon, one broke away and it was still going when we last saw it. It was about 2.5 miles away then still going north. We dont know if the observers jumped out with their parachutes or not.[43] They buried one of the aviatores here Sunday. He was a visitor. One of the aviators here took him up for a joy ride and they fell down. This was the first Saturday we were here. The pilot got killed and this fellow died last Friday. We played a concert there at the aviation [field] last Sunday. They have it swell over there.

We got 68 more men this week, and more coming right along

This apparent accident at Ft. Sill involving an observation balloon may have been the one Marland wrote about.

43. Artillery units, including Marland's, trained with observation balloons inflated with hydrogen or coal gas and balloonists who occupied attached willow and bamboo baskets. A cable, secured to a gasoline-powered winch typically bolted to a heavy truck, was attached to the balloon. As its line played out, the balloon soared quickly about thirty feet per second, with the basketed-balloonists—a two-man crew was common—dangling beneath. By signaling with radios or flags, the aerialists reported on enemy movements and directed artillery fire. Enemy aircraft pilots viewed the spy balloons as an important target and acted accordingly. Casualty rates among observers were high despite the parachutes they carried. Their highly inflammable hydrogen-filled craft, when ignited, fell quickly from the sky. The Western Front Association, "Observation Balloons on the Western Front," May 22, 2008, http://www.westernfrontassociation.com.

so we will soon be filled up. Yesterdays paper said we should be in France Sept 15. I hope its so. I don't think we will go to Siberia by the latest report. They say the 8th division is going there. They are not quite ready and they are sending all those ready to France now. Our Regement belongs to the 34th Division so when you read and thing [anything] about the 34th they mean us to.

I am glad you folks are having such a good time. What will Pearly say when he hears the fellow next door takes you riding in his car. Well have a good time. Us fellows did not know how good we had it when we were home.

So you think I might feed the fishes, I doubt if we will have much to feed them in case we do. You know its different to travel in the army.

Well like you said news is scarce so will close
Marland
Will return the picture too. Its sure a dandy.
Say you are getting to be quiet a cook to I must say.

KNIGHTS OF COLUMBUS
WAR ACTIVITIES

Camp Fort Sill Okla
Aug 27 1918

Dear Sister and All

We are going to play a concert in 30 mineuts so thought I would write you a few lines while I am waiting. Every thing is the same. Still here. We wont know hardly any thing more about leaving now hardly till about a day or so before we go. I hope we get over soon. One of the boys in my tent had a letter from William Hulmquist. He went over in June and he said he had not seen Standley yet. He said the night be fore he wrote they all had to get in dug outs as the German areoplanes were making a raid over their camp.

I suppose you are all going out to the fair. Don't sunburn your throat watching areoplanes. They are flying like that every day here. So we don't think about them no more. I see the Korseland boy that lived across from Aunt Emmas got killed. The Germans shot his areoplane down. [Milo Franklin Korslund, 25, lived in St. Paul. He was killed in action April 12, 1918.]

I got thait cookies papa sent, Thanks they sure were good. So Mamma said them cloths were dirty. Maybe you will excuse me if I tell you how it was. I havent used them since long be fore we left cody as it was to warm. But I did not have no tight place to put them in. So when ever a dust storm come up they got full of dirk. And then when we got up here, we got orders one day to send them home the next so I did not get time to wash them again.

Have you taken any pictures yet. When you have some finished send them down so I can see them and then I will return them. If you get some good ones of Papa and Mamma I would like to take them a cross with me. I am sure I will see standley there and he is anxious to see any thing from home too. When you write him let him known where and what I am doing as he dont seem to get all my letters. Will have to quiet now.

With Love to All

Marland

★ ★ ★

"WITH THE COLORS"
YMCA

Fort Sill Okla.
Sunday Sept 8

Dear Sister and All.

I just had supper and there is nothing to do now so I thought I would write a few lines. I should of wrote sooner but we are kept so busy we havent hardley any time. Last night we played a concert at Lawton and after that we played a dance there.

Well we leave this week, possibly Wednesday. I will drop a line now and then along the road so you know where I am. You can use my same address for a while yet as they foreward the mail.

I am glad you got the Bonds. Tell Papa to use them if he wants to.

I suppose you have started school now. Well you want to Study hard. Tywriting auto come easy to you as your fingers are limber on acount of play piano. Is Jewel practising any. How about she take Standleys saxophone and practis alittle on it Thats a nice instrument for a girl.

I suppose you all took in the fair. [The Minnesota State Fair, held for 10 days late in summer.] Did you get a stiff neck looking at the areoplanes. We are so used to them now we hardley ever look at them.

I am going to send my razor home to morrow. We were all issued razors, shaving brush, comb and towels. We can only take what we put on our back. We have turned in almost every thing. all we have now is. one blanket, 2 shirts, 2 suits underwear. 4 pr socks, one woolen suit, one pair shoes, one blanket, overcoat, rain coat, and hat. They have turned in our rifles and pistols so we only have our pistol belt, water canteen, mess kit, and pack of our equipment left. We carrey our instruments too so I guess it will be load enough any how.

Have you heard from Standley lately. When you write you let him know where I am. I hope I will be able to find him soon.

So he thinks I will need a few more pockets. I will find room for junk alright. I suppose I will pick up a bunch of stuff, as its nice to have a few suveniers after the war is over.

I have a few pictures laying around here I will put them in this letter. When you take any new ones we are always glad to see them. Well news is scarce so will close with Love to All

Marland.

[Postcard with two one-cent stamps postmarked Lafayette, Indiana, addressed to Mr. Alvin Williams, 391 Arundel St, St Paul, Minn.]

Sat. Sept 14

Dear Folks. We are on our way now. We just left Decatur Ill. We were off there and had a march and then went to to [the] Y.M.CA and had a swim. It sure felt good to get a bath. We left Ft. Sill Thurs. Morning. I guess we will hit Detroit pretty soon. The country is pretty nice here. The corn is about the same as up north. The train shakes so [I] can hardly write. The Red Cross is awful good along the road. They are down by the train every place we stop and gave us drinks, apples, cookies, cigerretts and so on. We were off at Oklahoma City too and marched around. Its nice and cool now so its swell traveling Will write later so you know where I am.

Marland

[Postcard with color illustration, "First Baptist Church, Peru, Ind." with two one-cent stamps addressed to Miss Olga Williams, 391 Arundel St, St Paul, Minn., postmarked 15 September 1918.]

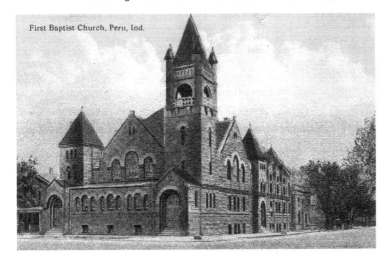

First Baptist Church, Peru, Ind.

Dear Sister.
We just left this place. We were off and played there. Its a fine country here. A little chilly now. We do not know where we are going yet.
Marland

[Postcard with color illustration "Main Street, Looking South from the Dudley, Salamanca, N.Y.," two one-cent stamps, addressed to Mr Alvin Williams, 391 Arundel St, St Paul, Minn., postmarked September 18, 1918.]

We were just off here and played. Are going to pull out now. Its 8.30 PM Sunday 15th. It is raining now. We will get to New York around 4 PM to morrow. am feeling fine.
Marland

MAIN STREET, LOOKING SOUTH FROM THE DUDLEY, SALAMANCA, N. Y.

[Envelope with a three-cent stamp addressed to Miss Olga Williams, 391 Arundel St, St. Paul, Minn.]

"WITH THE COLORS"
YMCA

Camp Upton L.I. N.Y.[44]
Sept 19–1918

Dear Sister and All.

I suppose you all have been waiting for a letter but we have been so busy that I havent had time. We are having inspections and things right after another all the time. Will have another in a few mineuts. We are also are getting our equipment all issued now. We are going to get our sea caps and work leggons this after noon.

This is a nice camp. There are about 50 000 here. We live in Barracks here where its pretty nice as we had a lot of rain here.

There is a lot of Spanish influenca here as I suppose you saw in the pape[r].[45] The Regiment next to us is quarnteened. They have about 200 case but not serious. I hope none of our boys get it as

44. In 1917, the U.S. Army ordered construction of Camp Upton on Long Island, New York, as an induction and training facility for World War I soldiers. Named after Major General Emory Upton, a Union general in the Civil War, the camp accommodated 37,000 soldiers. Irving Berlin, the famous songwriter of the period, was among the first soldiers in Camp Upton. He, along with all his comrades, loathed the morning bugle call, so he wrote the popular World War I song, "Oh How I Hate to Get Up in the Morning." It became an instant hit. Brookhaven National Laboratory, "Camp Upton," https://www.bnl.gov/about/history/campupton.php. See also, http://longislandgenealogy.com/CampUpton.html.

45. Marland refers to the influenza epidemic of 1918–1919 that was now underway. It grew into a global disaster, the most deadly in human history. *The Influenza Pandemic of 1918–1919,* Stanford University, https://virus.stanford.edu/uda/.

Panoramic view of Camp Upton, Long Island, New York

that would hold us here 3 weeks. We expect to leave next week.

We had a fine trip. We saw quiet abit of new York as we came over. Its almost as big as St Paul. We also had a nice ride on the Ferry over to the Island. We saw two Transports leaving, and also a number of battle ships. There was a big Swedish Liner too.

Remount stations provided horses for U.S. Army units. Horses at Camp Upton were destined for France.

We might move down to camp Mills in a day or so. This camp is 60 Miles from New York.[46]

I have not received any Mail from home yet. So I hope you will write soon. I have to get busy now. So good by Love to all Marland

Write soon

46. The War Department set up three Long Island embarkation points—camps Mills, Merritt, and part of Upton—to facilitate movement of troops to France. Camp Mills was about twenty miles from New York City harbor. James A. Huston, *The Sinews of War: Army Logistics, 1775–1953* (Washington D. C.: Center of Military History, United States Army, 1997) 345–347.

★ ★ ★

"WITH THE COLORS"
YMCA

Sept. 23 1918.

Dear Daddy Mother, and all.

Will write you a few lines to night and let you know I am feeling fine. Every thing is fine here. I have been pretty busy all day.

The U.S. Army created Camp Upton on New York's Long Island in 1917 as a final training facility for U.S. troops soon departing for France. These soldiers are conducting a bayonet drill.

We have had a lot of rain here and its been a little cold too. I suppose its getting a little chilly in St Paul also.

We are all well equiped now. Ready to see the Huns if we are able to catch them. They are running pretty fast I see.

This will be the last letter I will write on this side I think so if you dont hear for a couple, three, weeks don't worry. You can write right allong thou as I will get all mail writen to this address I put in the bottom of this letter. Hoping this will find you all well I will close with Love to All

Marland.

Would write more but am not allowed too.

Write to this address.

Musc. Marland R. Williams

125U.S.F.A. Band

via New York. A.E. F. [American Expeditionary Forces]

Am holding the paper on my lap so its kind of hard writing[47]

47. Marland's unit boarded the SS *Saxon* that day. "Am holding the paper on my lap" could indicate his hurry to dash off one last letter home before shipping out. There were no guarantees he would survive the ocean crossing, and he couldn't be certain that he'd be able to send letters from France once he got there. Lt. Harvey Johnson, "Company L," *Goodhue County in the World War* (Red Wing, MN: Red Wing Printing Co., 1919) 183–184.

Finally Going Across

[Marland Williams, conversation recorded by his son, Gerald Williams,
November 1991 Cassette 3, possession of the Editor]

Marland was among the two million U.S. soldiers who sailed by troopship to France and the war. He recorded the following account of his unit's crossing the Atlantic Ocean when he was 92 years old.

"After a short time of training there [Fort Sill] we were sent to Camp Upton on Long Island and made ready for overseas. We were all anxious to get on the boats and get across, not realizing what we were getting into. On the way over, our boat—an old Irish cattle boat [SS Saxon]—was our home for fourteen days. We were a convoy of fourteen boats, and as we approached the North Sea we ran into a terrific storm—almost a hurricane force. And one of the boats was struck by another one of the convoy and sank. There were many casualties on this boat. It was fortunate that it was mostly equipment on that boat and did not have the large accompaniment of men that most of the boats had. One night we got the word that a boat was torpedoed just a short way behind us. It had passed us just a short time before, going back to New York, so we were in the proximity of the submarines. There was a continual virgil [sic] on the boat watching, and no lights were allowed. You couldn't even smoke a cigarette on the boat, afraid that they might detect the light.

"This was during the flu epidemic and we had twenty-one deaths on our boat going over dying from the flu. Our Medical Major died on the way, and one nurse. They died very close to the landing in Liverpool so they were taken into Liverpool, and the other nineteen were dropped into the sea. This was sad to see your friends, one after the other, wrapped up in canvas and some coal added, and dumped overboard so they would sink. It was with a sigh of relief that we landed at Liverpool and could step on dry land again. From there we took a train across England.

"After we got to France we were taken to a rest camp for a day, given clean clothing and went through a de-louser, as everybody—or so many of the fellows—developed lice in the service. And then we had a shower, and made our skin all soaped up, the water was shut off and we had to leave the shower.

"After this we were taken to a chateau at Cussac, France. Here we stayed for three days, got organized, and then our regiment was divided up into different units, and as necessary these units were taken up to the front lines. I forgot to mention, one afternoon while we were in England we were asked to play for a royal reception at some notable home. The grounds were like a big park and the building was beautiful. One thing I'll always remember there, that the bathrooms all had mirrors for ceilings."

[Envelope with three one-cent stamps addressed to Mr. Alvin Williams,
391 Arundel St, St. Paul, Minn.]

ARMY AND NAVY
YOUNG MEN'S CHRISTIAN ASSOCIATION
"WITH THE COLORS"

Some where on the Atlantic
Oct 5. 1918

Dear Folks

Will write you a few lines and let you know I am feeling fine. I was a little sick the first day out, but got over it soon. Just about every body were a little sick.

The waters have been kind of rough all the time, but we are used to the rocking now.

I did not see Benny in [Camp] upton as he had left already.[48] You tell Standley I am over when you write so he knows it.

We can not write much now because we are not allowed to so will close

With Love to All

Marland

Musc. Marland R. Williams

125 F.A. Band

via N.Y. A.E.F.

[Censored by] Theodore S. Cox, Capt. U.S.A

[Printed at bottom of page] "To the Writer: Save by Writing on Both Sides of this Paper. To the Folks at Home: Save Food, Buy Liberty Bonds and War Savings Stamps."

SOLDIERS' MAIL.

THE AMERICAN RED CROSS

MILITARY POST OFFICE SOLDIERS MAIL

NO POSTAGE NECESSARY.

THIS SIDE FOR ADDRESS ONLY.

Mr Alvin Williams
391 Arundel St
St Paul
Minn

THE SHIP ON WHICH I SAILED HAS ARRIVED SAFELY OVERSEAS.

Name Marland R. Williams
Organization 125 F.A. Band
American Expeditionary Forces.

Parents worried about the safety of their sons and daughters crossing the Atlantic to France were relieved to get this simple but clear message.

48. Camp Upton was one of three embarkation camps controlled by the New York Port of Embarkation during the war. It was located in Yaphank on Long Island near Camp Mills and had capacity for 18,000 troops.

★ ★ ★

[Envelope addressed to Mr. Alvin Williams, 391 Arundel St, St. Paul, Minn., U.S.A.;
stamped A.E.F. PASSED AS CENSORED A. 3640.]

AMERICAN Y.M.C.A.
ON ACTIVE SERVICE WITH THE
AMERICAN EXPEDITIONARY FORCE

Some Where in France[49]
Sun. Oct 27 1918.

Dear Folks.

Will write you a few lines to night and let you know I am feeling fine and like dandy over here.

We are staying in bittets [billets—temporary quarters] and have a swell place. Every thing is nice and green here and the weather is quiet warm. We have rain every other day here, but the roads are all hard so it don't get very muddy.

We are pretty busy playing now. We have a concert every after noon except Saterdays. The French people sure enjoy music. Our Band Leader gets flowers all- most every concert.

The 125th Field Artillery Band gathered for a concert in an unnamed French city.

The French people are fine. They do every thing they can and more. There is not a French man here of military age that is not in the army[50]. The only ones at home are those discharged on account of disability.

49. Soldiers were not allowed to make specific references to their location for security reasons.

50. France, a nation of 40 million in 1914, had suffered terribly. By late October 1918, it was nearing 1.3 million soldiers dead. *"War Losses (France)"*, International Encyclopedia of the First World War, http://encyclopedia.1914-1918-online.net/article/war_losses_france.

Things are quiet high here. The people can not buy hardly any sweets. The people over [in the] U.S. don't [know] what war is till they have seen a few effects of it.

I have not seen Standly yet. I have wrote to him, so expect [an] answer pretty soon. I talked with a boy from his regiment and he said he would look him up as soon as he got back.

There is a lot of things I would like to write but can not. so will have a lot to tell when I get home. I have not got my mail from home yet so am waiting for a letter. So I hope you will write often. It is harder for mail to go back so dont worry if you do not hear very often. So will close with Love to all

Marland

Musc. Marland R. Williams

125 F.A. Band Hq. Co.

France

via N.Y. American Ex. Forces

[Censored by] Theodore S. Cox, Capt. U.S.A.

[Envelope addressed to Mr. Alvin Williams, 391 Arundel St., St. Paul, Minn. U.S.A.; stamped A.E.F. PASSED AS CENSORED A. 3640; O.K.]

AMERICAN Y.M.C.A.
ON ACTIVE SERVICE WITH THE
AMERICAN EXPEDITIONARY FORCE

Some where in France

Oct 31 1918

Dear Folks.

Will write you a few lines this morning and let you know I am feeling fine and that I received yours and Olgas letter of the 22nd and 29 of Sept Yesterday. I also got one from Elmie Strom.[51] It

51. The Strom family also attended First Lutheran Church in St. Paul. John and Matilda Strom and Marland's parents decided their children would make a good couple, and encouraged Elmie to write to Marland. Apparently the parents were correct, because Marland and Elmie began dating after he returned from the war. They were married at First Lutheran Church in St. Paul on August 11, 1923. See "Life After the War" for more about Marland and Elmie.

sure is nice to get mail now. I have not heard from Standley yet but have written him a couple three letters.

The fellows are drilling hard and we are playing every day, so we are kept busy.

The weather is nice and warm yet. Altho I guess the winters are about as nice here. There is a lot of things I would like to write but can not. so will have so much more to tell you when I get home.

The svea boys are still with us. They are all well. I hear William Hulmquist is only a few miles from here, so I might have chances to see him. You know he left last summer and has been at the front allready.

I don't think the war will last so very long now, the way things look here.

Tell Olga she is doing fine with her type writing. Well will close with Love to all

Marland

Musc. Marland R. Williams

125 F.A. Band Hq. Co.

France

via N.Y. American Ex. Forces

[Censored by] Theodore S. Cox, Capt., U.S.A. [and] O.K.

Censored by H.F. Hofflander, 1st Lt. U.S.A.

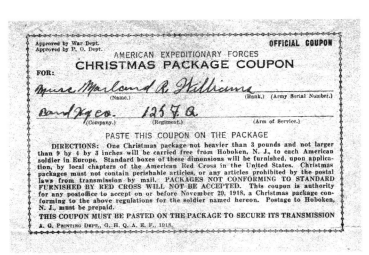

Christmas packages for overseas soldiers were to be sent "on or before November 20, 1918."

★ ★ ★

AMERICAN Y.M.C.A.
ON ACTIVE SERVICE WITH THE
AMERICAN EXPEDITIONARY FORCE

Nov 23 1918
Some where in France

Dear Folks.

Will write you a few lines and let you know I am feeling fine. I received your letters of the 13 and 23 the other day, but as we have moved since that I have had no chance to write. That picture was swell of Jewel. She sure has grown. I wont know the girls when I get home.

The war news is pretty good now and I think we will be home quiet soon. I have not heard from Standley yet, but I think he will beat me home.

We are at a fine place now. The weather is little colder here and its not very much fun to play out side.

The French people were sure happy when the armitint [armistice] was signed.[52] They celebrated over a week. There is a lot I would like to say but can not. So will have all the more to tell when I get back. I had a letter from Sidney. Have Olga drop him a line and let hi know I got it and will write later.

so will close with love to all
Marland.
Musc. Marland R. Williams
125 F.A. Band Hq. Co.
American Ex. Forces
France
via N.Y.
O.K. D. Jacobson, 2ⁿᵈ Lt. U.S.A.

---

52. The term "armistice" means a cessation of hostilities as a prelude to peace negotiations that ended the fighting. The November 11, 1918, armistice brought an end to the fighting. The 1919 Paris Peace Conference produced the World War's formal conclusion. Ironically for Marland and his artillery regiment, the shooting stopped as they reached the front. They had been in the army for about twenty months.

Marland is Missing

The 125th Field Artillery Regiment remained at Medoc, France, until Christmas Day 1918, when they sailed for America. Marland's unit was later discharged at Camp Dodge, Iowa, and the men left for their homes. His family went to meet the train when it reached St. Paul. Marland's euphonium was on board, but he was not. His buddies only knew that he was kept in France because he was sick.

Marland had contracted Spanish influenza and pneumonia. He was held in a French hospital to convalesce and avoid infecting others on the ship. (See Stanley's letter of January 15, 1919.) Alvin returned to the station daily, expecting to see his son step off the train. It is not difficult to imagine the family's increasing dread as another day passed with no news of Marland.

The newspaper clipping at right was taped to the inside front cover of Marland's album. It ran on page one of the *St. Paul Pioneer Press* on January 31, 1919.

In 2016, Marland's Army uniform was to be displayed in an exhibit. Before it was lent, the pockets were checked. Three things were found: an inspection slip from the garment manufacturer, a rosette of red, yellow, and blue satin ribbons, and a theater ticket stub. These seemingly insignificant items provided a clue to what happened to Marland after he returned to the U.S.

According to Marland's Military Service Record, he arrived in Hoboken, New Jersey, on January 19, 1919. He may have continued his recovery at the post hospital at Camp Merritt in Cresskill, New Jersey, but the camp commander's negative response suggests Marland was elsewhere.

The ticket stub for the 44th Street Theater in New York is dated January 21, 1919. Only two days after Marland arrived stateside, he took in a Broadway play! The show was "Little Simplicity," a musical comedy set in 1912 in Tunis, Africa, then Paris, and finally somewhere in France in 1917.

DODGED CASUALTY LISTS, NOW MISSING IN U. S.

Private Marland Williams, son of Mr. and Mrs. Alvin Williams, 62 Summit avenue west, escaped the army casualty lists while he was in France, but now he is missing in his own country.

For nearly two weeks his parents have been sending telegrams and making inquiries in the hope of learning his whereabouts in the United States. They have at last appealed to the War Camp Community Service.

Mr. Williams has learned that his son, who was in the One Hundred and Twenty-fifth field artillery, left France about two weeks later than the rest of the division.

A telegram was received January 19 from the Salvation Army saying that he had reached New York that day and had gone to Camp Merritt. A telegram to the commandant at Camp Merritt brought back the information that the missing soldier had not been there.

It is feared that Private Williams is seriously ill in some army hospital.

Marland saw this show ten days before the St. Paul paper reported him missing. Perhaps because long-distance communication was neither inexpensive nor easy, an eighteen-year old young man did not think to let his family know his whereabouts while he experienced some of New York City before returning home.

Forwarded 9/3/20. Approved by H.R.Packard Capt Inf for
Victory Medal with clasp.

ENLISTMENT RECORD.

Name: *Marland R. Williams* Grade: *Musician 2nd Class*

Enlisted, or ~~Inducted~~, *April, 30, ,1917, at Duluth, Minnesota*

Serving in *First* enlistment period at date of discharge.

Prior service:* *None*

Noncommissioned officer: *No*

Marksmanship, gunner qualification or rating: † *None*

Horsemanship: *Not mounted*

Battles, engagements, skirmishes, expeditions: *American Expeditionary Force France*

Knowledge of any vocation: *Student*

Wounds received in service: *None*

Physical condition when discharged:
Triple
Typhoid prophylaxis completed *August, 6, 1917*
Triple
Paratyphoid prophylaxis completed *September 24, 1917*

Married or single: *Single*

Character: *Excellent*

Remarks: *No A.W.O.L. No absence under G.O. 31
W.D. 1912 or G.O. 45 W.D. 1914. Due travel pay
from Camp Grant Illinois.*

Signature of soldier: *Marland R. Williams*

CAMP GRANT, ILL. FEB 1919

PAID IN FULL $ 56.01

ALEX. C. McKELVEY,
Capt. Q. M. Corps.

2nd LIEUT. Q. M. C.

Commanding 10th Co.

*Give company and regiment or corps or department, with inclusive dates of service in each enlistment.
†Give date of qualification or rating and number, date, and source of order announcing same.

3—3164

Honorable Discharge from The United States Army

TO ALL WHOM IT MAY CONCERN:

This is to Certify, That *Marland R. Williams #1,430,481

*Musician 2nd Class, Headquarters Company, 125th Field Artillery

THE UNITED STATES ARMY, as a Testimonial of Honest and Faithful

Service. is hereby Honorably Discharged from the military service of the

P.P. 8   S.O. For the convenience of the Government

United States by reason of Hqrs. Camp Grant, Illinois Feb. 1st 1919

Said   Marland R. Williams   was born

in Trenton   , in the State of Wisconsin

When enlisted he was 18 years of age and by occupation a Student

He had Blue eyes, Light hair, Light complexion, and

was 5 feet 9 inches in height.

Given under my hand at Camp Grant, Illinois this

5 day of February, one thousand nine hundred and nineteen

Washington, D.C. APR 10 1919
Paid: $60 under Act of Congress approved
February 24th, 1919.

C. E. GRAY,
Major, Q. M. Corps.

Major Infantry M. S. A.
Commanding.

Form No. 525, A. G. O.
Oct. 9-18.

2—5154

*Insert name, Christian name first; e. g., "John Doe."
†Insert Army serial number, grade, company and regiment or arm or corps or department; e. g., "1,620,302"; "Corporal, Company A, 1st Infantry"; "Sergeant, Quartermaster Corps"; "Sergeant, First Class, Medical Department."
‡If discharged prior to expiration of service, give number, date, and source of order or full description of authority therefor.

Lawrence Stanley Williams, Battalion Sergeant Major
Headquarters Company, 151st Field Artillery, Rainbow Division

Letters from Stanley

Lawrence Stanley Williams, a 21-year-old St. Paul bank clerk, enlisted in the Minnesota National Guard's 1st Field Artillery on April 23, 1917.

When taken into the federal army in August, the Minnesota Guard unit was designated the 151st Field Artillery and assigned to what emerged as the nation's most celebrated combat unit of the war, the 42nd "Rainbow" Division. Organized to represent nearly every part of the country, Rainbow included units from 26 states. To the elation of its members, the 151st F. A. became Minnesota's representative in the division. The artillery contingent reached France in October 1917 and commenced final training.[53]

Stanley (he preferred his middle name) Williams received corporal's stripes while still in the U.S. and was later promoted to Battalion Sergeant Major in the 2nd Battalion's Headquarters Company. That advancement made him one of the regiment's highest ranking noncommissioned officers. Stanley, and brother Marland as well, had attended Red Wing Seminary, a secondary school in Red Wing, Minnesota. Stanley's education and experience with banking contributed to his advancement.

From February through May 1918, the 151st F. A. suffered losses during exchanges with enemy artillery batteries. In June the unit was involved in heavy, costly fighting while supporting division infantry at Chateau-Thierry and breaking the German line at St. Mihiel. The massive Meuse-Argonne offensive followed, and the 151st and Battalion Sgt. Major Williams took active part in it all.[54]

Following the November 11 armistice, the Rainbow Division and other units marched into a subdued Germany. In spring 1919 the weary veterans were ordered home, reaching the United States on April 25. Williams was with the 151st when it arrived in St. Paul on May 8.[55]

53. Louis L. Collins, "History of the 151st Field Artillery, Rainbow Division" in *Minnesota in the World War* (St. Paul: Minnesota War Records Commission, 1924) 5–20. Harold S. Johnson, *Roster of the Rainbow Division* (New York: Eaton & Gettinger, 1917), see "151st Regiment (1st Minnesota) Field Artillery, Battery C," 191.

54. "151st Field Artillery, Rainbow Division," *Northwest Warriors Magazine*, 1/3 (August 1919) 21, 60. For maps and a description of the American advance at St. Mihiel and Meuse-Argonne offensive, see Vincent J. Esposito, *The West Point Atlas of American Wars*, (New York: Praeger, 1959) 2: 68–70.

55. Collins, "History of the 151st Field Artillery," 165–190.

★ ★ ★

Camp Mills, L.I., New York
10/4/17.

Dear Folks:

Will drop you a few lines and let you know that I have not left yet. Expect to go within four or five days but no one will know when we leave. I have it pretty easy now, all I do is take care of ordnance records [military weapons—cannons, artillery, and ammunition] and help the clerk and drill when I feel like doing something. I have never felt better in my life. I am only waiting for the day to come when we can start. After this when addressing be sure and write like this:

Battery "C" 151st F.A.
42nd Division[56]
American Expeditionary Forces
After we leave the U.S. this would reach me any place in the world.

I hear Marland regiment is now Artillery and I'm glad because it is a better branch of the service and less danger. From what I under-stand we will go so much training over there that we may not even be in on the next spring drive. Well everything is the same and I do not know of any news, so will close for this time with love to all. Will try a[nd] drop a line when we leave the U.S., so goodbye from your big boy

Stanley.

Over the Top *with the* **Rainbow Division**

This image from a magazine article ad capitalizes on the Rainbow Division's fame. Stars on the map show from which states its regiments came.

56. Minnesota National Guard's 1st Field Artillery regiment was renamed the 151st Field Artillery when absorbed into the Regular Army. To the elation of the Minnesotans, their unit was assigned to the 42nd "Rainbow" Division. That outfit emerged as the nation's most celebrated combat contingent of the Great War. The Rainbow nickname developed because its regiments came from all over the nation. The 42nd Rainbow's Minnesota-based 151st F. A. reached France in October 1917. Adjutant General [Minnesota], *A History of the Minnesota National Guard* (St. Paul: 1940) 16–17. U.S. Army Center of Military History, "151st Field Artillery Regiment (First Minnesota Heavy Artillery)" http://www. history.army.mil.

P.S. Say I am going to make an allotment to you of $25.00 [$397] per month and you can put it in the bank for me. In this way the Government will send it to you and will not send it accross to us over there, and I will not have to send it back. The first one will not come for about a month, tho,.

★ ★ ★

Camp Mills, L.I., N.Y.[57]
Oct. 13th, 1917.

Dear Folks:

Will write you a few lines and let you know that I am still At Camp Mills, L.I., but expect to leave at any time, but the exact time is not known and could not give it even if I wanted to on account of the censor.

I have received your letters and I have written at least once or twice a week mostly twice, so my letters must of got lost or held up. Hereafter I will number my letters, this being one, the next two etc. and you will know whether or not you get them all. Of course you know after we get started I can not write so many and it will take a long time for them to get there.

We got paid yesterday and I am enclosing twenty five dollars which you can put in the bank for me. I wrote in one of my letters that I had made an allotment of twentyfive dollars a month to you and for you to put it in the bank for me. I do not know if you have received that letter or not but the Government will send you twenty five dollars a month from me and you can put it in the bank for me. The fellow in Window #13 has my book, Papa knows where it is. [Before he enlisted, Stanley worked as a clerk at Merchant Bank in St. Paul.]

I am having a good time, not working very much as I am in the office most of the time and I can eat from the time I get up till I go to bed. Tomorrow I am invited out to dinner by a family in Freeport. The people around here treat us very nice. It gets pretty

57. Camp Mills soon advertised itself as "The Birthplace of the 42nd Rainbow Division." The Minnesotans were among the first regiments to reach the five-week-old military base. Nassau County Long Island, "Historic Hempstead Plains: Camp Mills Training Camp, Embarkation Camp and Debarkation Camp, (1917–1919)."

cold down here now during the night, and [I] will be glad when we can move, we will have extensive training when we get accross.

You say that Marland says he has not heard from me, well I have written to him every once in the while, just as much as he has written to me. Suppose you are about ready to move now and I am waiting for the time when the war will be over and I can come home to Papa and Mamma. [Stanley's parents and sisters had moved from Trenton, Wisconsin, to St. Paul.]

Wrote a letter to Mr. Fairchild of the Mer. Bank and hinted about getting my job back and yesterday I got an answer and he said he thought they would be lucky if they got me back, so I guess that sounds pretty good. They still think I am a Sgt. Maj. Sgt. Phillips has given his folks the address of all the boys folks who are in this regiment and they intend to get together and do what they can for the boys in the organization. Their address is 683 Plum St. so if you hear from them you know what it is. Well I have all I want and everything is fine and not knowing anything else to write will close for this time with lots of love

From Stanley.

Oct. 18th 3 P.M.
On Board Ship President Lincoln

Dear Folks

Will write you a few lines

We broke camp this morning at 7⁰⁰ o clock and went right to this ship[58] The old Fatherland is right along side of us and we are in the harbor now Think that we will leave tonight

There are 5000 Soldiers aboard and it certainly is some crowd

I do not know how soon you will recieve this but I expect it will be a long time before you get any more they might hold this on acc't of censors until we arrive in France We got our orders last night, but

58. Stanley's unit was the first to take the former German-owned steamer *President Lincoln* to France. Ten years old, the *Lincoln* was a combination passenger-cargo vessel. On May 31, 1918, German submarine U-90 sent three torpedoes into the ship, sinking it in 20 minutes. It was the largest U.S. naval vessel sunk during the war. "Ships Hit During WWI: President Lincoln," uboat.net, http://uboat.net/wwi/ships_hit/4905. html accessed December 8, 2016.

they did not tell any of the men except the 1st Sgt and me and the clerk We got up at three woke the rest and got ready and left at 3.

Well I do not know of anything to write so with the best of love to all write and tell Marland I am

Your Big Boy

Stanley

Somewhere in France
Nov. 20, 1917

My Dear Sister + Folks

I have just recieved my first mail over here and it is one letter dated Oct 18 in which you say that you are packing.

We are now in a camp in a very pretty part of France and when out you can see the French people farming with their oxen teams, and apples piled very much all over.

I can go out and pick Holly and evergreen right outside of our camp and it is the prettiest I have ever seen as it comes right off the trees fresh.

You want to read the Leslies and Colliers Magazines and you can find out and see pictures of how it is over here. Will tell you all about every thing when I get back home which I hope will be soon. I have not heard from Marland yet. Tell him to write soon.

I suppose you are all settled now in your new home and hope you like it fine only wish I could be home for Xmas. Thanksgiving will be here soon. Have not seen any snow yet. Have you. Say when you write let me know if the Gov. sends the allotment and I also took Insurance for Ten Thousand Let me know what you have heard from them. This Ins is something like accident Ins. Did you get the $25^{00} [$397] I sent while in Camp Mills?

Well this is all I can write so will close with Love to all and write soon and often[59] from

Stanley.

59. The 151st F. A. landed at St. Nazaire, France, on October 31, 1917, and headed toward Coëtquidan, a training base in Brittany.

Weapons of 151st Field Artillery

In mid-November 1917, the men of the 151st U.S. Field Artillery first made the acquaintance of "Mademoiselle Soixante-quinze" [Miss 75] and were enchanted. Supplied by their French comrades, these 75mm field guns proved easier to handle than the American cannons on which they had trained.[60]

Americans liked the quick firing soixante-quinze—15 rounds per minute at a range up to four miles. Its innovative recoil system and easy-to-operate breech resulted in swifter, smoother operation. The 75s fired modest-sized projectiles—12.3-pound high explosives and 16-pound shrapnel shells. The 151st also made good use of the four-ton French-made 155mm Schneider Howitzer, a piece that fired a 100-pound shell.[61]

The 151st F. A. received specific battlefield tasks. Among the most common: counter battery barrages designed to knock out enemy artillery; creeping barrages, a wall of protective fire that directly preceded friendly infantry units as they advanced; and box barrage, artillery fire that surrounded a target area and then destroyed soldiers and weapons trapped inside.[62]

Although there were no safe jobs on the war's Western Front, artillerists fared better than infantrymen. The 151st F. A. sustained 23 killed in action or dead from wounds, 25 who died of disease or accident, and 441 who were victims of poison gas.[63]

Photograph showing 151st F. A. gun crews and the proper positioning of men and weapons

60. Collins, *History of the 151st Field Artillery*, 26 [quote], 209–210. Not to be outdone with heavier weapons, Battery C was also first in 155mm howitzer tests.

61. First Division Museum at Cantigny, "French 75mm Field Gun," http://www.firstdivisionmuseum.org/museum/exhibits/tankpark/75mm.aspx and "155mm French Schneider Howitzer," http://www.firstdivision-museum.org/museum/exhibits/tankpark/155mm.aspx.

62. Niall Ferguson, *The Pity of War: Explaining World War I* (New York: Basic Books, 1999) 303–310.

63. Collins, *History of the 151st Field Artillery*, 407.

BATTERY "C" 151ST FIELD ARTILLERY
AMERICAN EXPEDITIONARY FORCES
FRANCE

December 19th, 1917.

Dear Folks:

Will now write you a few lines in reply to your letter of the 7th which I received last night. I had almost given up hope of receiving any as I had not heard from you for quite awhile and some of the boys have received mail sent as late as the 27th of Nov. I have never felt better than I do now and everything is fine, saw the first snow last night and the ground only freezes over night so you can imagine how colds it gets here, have very fine barracks and I am doing the same work as before.

I am glad to hear that you like your new place and am waiting for the day when I can [come] home and be with you all again, is Marland still in Camp Cody, or are they coming accross also. Say the last two or three times that I wrote I asked you to let me know if you received any of my letters, that is give the date I wrote them and also if your got the $25.00 [$397] Post Office Order I sent from Camp Mills, L.I., [and] the $25.00 per month allotment that I made? It works like this, every month they deduct $25.00 on the pay roll and send it to you, you can keep it for me or use it if you wish. I also took out a $10,000 [$158,945] W.R. Life Ins. with the Government, and now when you write let me know if you have heard anything regarding this.[64]

I suppose you know what this day of the month is to me, and so far it looks pretty good. [Stanley's 22nd birthday was December 19th.] About a week ago I got a letter from a Lady in Minneapolis. I do not know where she got my name but suppose they have the names of everybody some place and she said that she was going to send me a Xmas Box and today it came. There was a knit sweater, gauntlets and a fine knit scarf, ciggerattes candy, and quite a few different

---

64. The War Risk Insurance Act, enacted in 1914, established a Bureau of War Risk within the Treasury Department to insure vehicles and individuals being shipped during World War I. Archive.org, "The War Risk Insurance Act," https://archive.org/stream/jstor-1822411/1822411_djvu.txt provides detail on this law, accessed December 27, 2016.

things, If you send anything over, send some candy, that is choco-
late bars, or something like that that will keep and not break up, you
can also send some cigars if you want to. I suppose Papa will not
like this, but it is better to use them than <u>something</u> else, which I do
not do. Well you know that I cant write much so will close for this
time with love to all, hoping you will have a merry Xmas and that I
will be there a year from now I am

    Stanley.

    [Censored by] Lt GC Neusen, 151 FA

Front and back covers for a Christmas 1917 musical program for "Minnesota's Best," the 151st F. A.

December 23rd, 1917.

Dear Papa, Mamma and all:

    Will write you a few more lines today as this is Sunday and have
nothing else to do. Received your letter of the 30th, had one of
our cooks translate mamma's note.[65] This one and one written the
7th are the ones written in Nov. that I have received and the Xmas

---

65. Stanley's mother, Hulda, probably wrote something in her native Swedish.

Package. I cannot use it now but will later and it certainly was fine. Xmas mail is coming in every day, we are also getting packages from the Mpls Journal and some other sources. What goes best is mostly candy, tobacco and little things like that. American goods are pretty scarce in this country.

There are a lot of things I would like to write about and it being Xmas you cannot imagine how lonesome it seems to be so far away, but hope that it will be different next Xmas. I like it fine otherwise and we have it good. Had beefsteak, fired [sic] onions mashed potatoes, coffee and bread for dinner. Xmas we will have turkey, Mince Pie and everything that goes with it, and other days we have good [food] to eat we also have the best cook in the regiment. Why don't Marland write me a letter, I have not heard from him since coming over. Well will close for this time with love to all and please write often and let me know if you get my letters, from

Stanley.

P.S. If you send anything, send a couple boxes of dark tan shoe polish. cannot get it here.

[Censored by] Lt GC Neusen, 151 FA

BATTERY "C" 151ˢᵀ FIELD ARTILLERY
AMERICAN EXPEDITIONARY FORCES
FRANCE

January 31ˢᵗ, 1918.

Dear Folks:

Will now write you a few lines and let you know that I am still alive and feeling better than ever. We are having what you would call late spring weather and during spare hours the boys are playing ball etc., I suppose you are wadding in the snow and complaining about the cold. There is a lot of things that I would like to write about but as I cannot write it I will have to wait till I get back which I hope will be before the snow flies again.

I received two letters today one written the 27ᵗʰ and Jan. 2ⁿᵈ, also two a couple of days ago. Olga says that you are receiving my allotment. It will have to be changed some now and it may be some time between a couple of them for the month of February and March but when you write let me know as often as you get them. I bought a #2A Brownie Camera and will send you a couple of pictures of myself as soon as I get them printed. I am now out with the Battery as Caisson Corporal and like it fine, have a horse of my own to ride.

As I was writing this I just received two more of your letters of the 10th and 13th so you see some of the mail is quite late in getting here. I am very glad that you like your place so well and that you having such a good time, I know you didn't have much enjoyment at Svea. Well I will have to close now, will write more in a couple of days, so with love to all I am

Corp Stanley L Williams

Bat. C 151st FA[66]

A.E. F Via New York

[Censored by] Everett F McCoy, 2 Lt 151 FA

On duty in France, Stanley Williams, left, is pictured with a comrade. Williams became a Battalion Sergeant Major while serving with the 151st Field Artillery.

Combat Operations February–March 1918

For security reasons, Stanley could not mention his regiment's location. The 151st moved to the Baccarat Sector of the front lines in February and set up headquarters at Lunéville, in the Lorraine region of France. The Minnesotans endured German shelling that included poison gas bombardments. They were still in the Lunéville area when Stanley wrote this letter. Source: "151st Field Artillery," *Northwest Warriors Magazine*, (March 1920): 21, 60.

66. Battery C was emerging as the best outfit in the 151st F. A. It placed first in proficiency among 11 units using 75mm guns and first of five in use of 155mm howitzers. Collins, *History of the 151st Field Artillery*, 209–210.

HEADQUARTERS SECOND BATTALION, 151ST F. A.
AMERICAN EXPEDITIONARY FORCES,
FRANCE.

April 7th, 1918.

Dear Folks at Home:

Will write you a few lines again, hoping this will find you all well, and let you know that I am still alive and feeling fine I suppose you have the last two or three letters I wrote, in one I enclosed 3 souvener handkerchiefs and I also sent you two copies of the Stars and Stripes newspaper printed by the A.E.F. Headquarters and in it you can get more news of what we are doing than I would be allowed to write. I also sent you a few A.E.F. cards, which I think explain themselves.

How is Marland, I got a letter from him about a month ago but have not heard since, suppose he will be on his way over soon, I do not think, that is if he comes over, that I will be able to see him unless I can see him when we get our weeks leave.

I received a letter from Rev. Grant and you can tell him for me that I am satisfied to join the Church where I have always went, that is the church I used to belong to and that I will not join his.

I am now in Headquarters Company, was made Battalion Sergeant Major dating April 6th and am with the 2nd Battalion. I have been with the 2nd Bn. now since Feb. 15th and I like it fine. [Stanley's promotion to Battalion Sergeant in the Headquarters Company placed him among the highest-ranking noncommissioned officers in the 151st F.A.]

I received your packages a couple of weeks ago and I also received another from the Bank. They certainly come in fine over here as we are unable to buy anything French that is any good at all. It is pretty nice here now, only it rains quite a bit and is a little chilly at times and also pretty noisy but am getting used to it now.

Well I cannot think of anything interesting to write so will close for this time with love to all.

From, Stanley.
L.S. Williams,
Bn. Sergt. Major, Headquarters Company,
151st Field Artillery, A.E.F.

Combat Operations, April 8

The regiment provided artillery support for a large "come and go" raid to take German prisoners. Batteries of the 151st fired a creeping barrage to open gaps in the enemy barbed wire. Source: Collins, *History of the 151st Field Artillery*, 219–220.

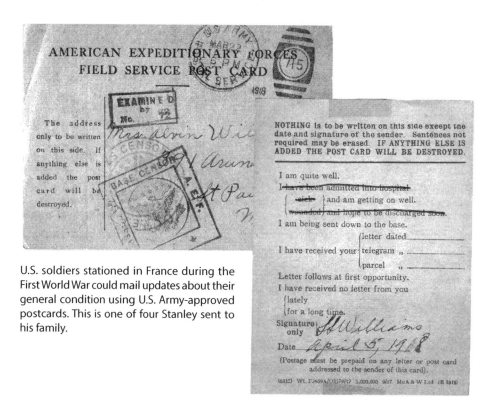

U.S. soldiers stationed in France during the First World War could mail updates about their general condition using U.S. Army-approved postcards. This is one of four Stanley sent to his family.

HEADQUARTERS SECOND BATTALION, 151ST F. A.
AMERICAN EXPEDITIONARY FORCES
FRANCE

April 14th, 1918.

Dear Folks:

Will write you a few lines again, letting you know that I am still alive and O.K. It is Sunday today and I have not done much except get out a few reports etc. This afternoon I took a walk around the country and it is getting to be pretty nice. We are billeted in small French towns, have quite a large room for office and I also sleep here and the men sleep in haylofts or whatever they are supposed to be. Over here the house, barn chicken coop and everything is one building,

Say, I wrote you a while ago to send me $25.00 [$397] and then to send me some every once in the while. But now that I have got promoted, which gives me about 55:00 [$874] per month, you do not need to send any but the $25.00. I also wish that you would send me a Safety Razor, get a cheap one as they are just as good for use when one is going from place to place and are not so easily lost. Also send me about ½ a dozen of sox, like the ones you sold for 3 pr for a quarter when you were at Hager [Wisconsin] as they are the best to wear now. The kind they issue are to big to suit me.

Received a letter from Marland a few days ago and I also wrote him one. Tell him that he doesn't want to be to anxious to leave where he is. I suppose he is getting to be [a] pretty good player now. I am glad to hear that you like where you are and that everything goes so good. I also hope that this war will end within the next four or five years so that I can come home again. I have lost all my ambition for Globe Trotting and when I get home, I will sure hang tight.

Well, I will have to close for this time hoping you are getting my letters, as I am writing 1 and 2 letters a week now, so with love to all, I am

Stanley.
Bn. Sgt. Maj. L.S. Williams, 2nd Bn. Hdqts., 151st F.A.
A.E.F., France.

★ ★ ★

HEADQUARTERS SECOND BATTALION, 151ST F. A.
AMERICAN EXPEDITIONARY FORCES,
FRANCE

May 4th, 1918.

Dear Folks:
Will write you a few lines again this evening. I am still alive and at it and everything is just about the same.

The last letter of yours that I received was dated the 8th of April but expect some mail soon. It does not come every day here, sometimes it is a week or two between.

About the only thing we get to keep our minds busy now is stories that circulate among the men, the latest is that we will be home for the 4th, hope it is true, but you know how rumors are. They say we are going to parade in Washington, also that we are going to take the place of 5 division on the border etc. I gues they think we are pretty good by that.

I see by one of your letters that Ted Swanson and Fredolf is over here, let me know what, Co., Reg. and Div. they are in and maybe I will run accross them sometime. Has Marland left yet, Tell him he is better off where he is.

Well, there is nothing new to write as we are treating the Boshe[67] the same as usual, only a little better at times, giving them lots of spare parts etc., so will close for this time with love to all.[68]

Stanley.

Bn.Sgt.Maj.L.S.Williams,

Hdqts. Co., 151st F.A.

Page topper from *Northwest Warriors Magazine*

Combat Operations, May 27

German artillery units opened a 10 p.m. bombardment of high explosives and poison gas that lasted until the next morning. The 151st started firing at the same time; the men at the guns endured wearing gas masks for hours. Germans continued intermittent gas shelling for several days. Source: Collins, *History of the 151st Field Artillery*, 54–55.

67. *Boche* is a derogatory French slang for the German army adopted by the British and Americans, said to have come from the word *caboche*, meaning "hard-headed" or "rascal." British Library, *World War One*, "Slang Terms at the Front," https://www.bl.uk/world-war-one/articles/slang-terms-at-the-front.

68. This refers to exchanges of artillery fire between the 151st F. A. and Germans. "Treating the Boshe the same as usual," means artillery fire, and "spare parts" indicates heavy explosives, gas, etc.

HEADQUARTERS SECOND BATTALION, 151ST F. A.
AMERICAN EXPEDITIONARY FORCES, FRANCE

May 29th, 1918.

Dear Folks:

The mail just arrived and I received your letter of May 7th and I have also received your of the 4th a couple of days ago. I am feeling fine except for a little cold and everything is going fine. Received a letter from Marland yesterday and I guess he is pretty anxious to get over here. It will be pretty good for him as they do not have very much to do.

I am enclosing another Stars and Stripes and will send one each week if you want me to, you can get a little idea of how things go in the army over here from this paper. I am also enclosing a couple of post cards of myself and Louie Campbell, Supply Sergt. In Battery "C" We were out one day and we had them taken but it is kind of poor. Will have some better ones taken when I can. I had a camera of my own, but we are not allowed to use them so it don't do me much good.

I am glad to hear that business is so good, and wish that I could be home to help, but I guess that will not be for a while yet, we have been here over 7 months now and hope by the end of 7 more that the Boche will have enough. The spare part throwing and air perfuming [poison gas] goes on just about the same from day to day.[69]

Well, there is nothing new to write about so will close for this time with love to all hoping that we will all be home together again soon, from

Stanley

Bn.Sgt.Maj.L.S.Williams,

151st Field Artillery.

---

69. Family members reported that Stanley was exposed to poison gas during his time in France and he suffered reduced lung capacity the rest of his life.

Combat Operations, June 15–July 5

The Rainbow (42nd) Division, including the 151st Field Artillery, was ordered to withdraw from the line and move to the endangered Champagne region. Stanley wrote this letter while the 151st and other artillery units waited to join the rest of the 42nd Division already transferred by train to Suippes. Artillery groups were in place by July 5. Source: Collins, "The Champagne Offensive," *History of the 151st Field Artillery*, 228-229.

HEADQUARTERS SECOND BATTALION, 151ST F. A. AMERICAN EXPEDITIONARY FORCES, FRANCE

July 3rd, 1918.

Dear Folks:

Will now write you a few lines and let you know that I am still alive and O.K. Received three of your letters yesterday but have not heard from Marland for quite a while. We have done some moving lately and while moving they do not accept outgoing mail so that is why I have not written before. I suppose you know where we were or what front as I sent you a couple of handkerchiefs with a cross on them. I am just beginning to find out what sunny France is as the sun sure does shine these days. and it certainly is a fine country around here. The people are all cutting hay etc. In this part they all seem to have up to date machinery and all the good machinery is American. Altho in some parts things are done in a very old fashioned way and everything is in little plots. Say when you write let me know what outfit Ted Swanson and Fridolph belong to and sometime I might happen to run accross them. There is a couple of boys in Bat. "C" now what came over as casuals that were in the 125th and left in March and they knew Marland well.[70] I understand that they can send packages now if requested so I am enclosing a request for some things and please send them tout de suite [at once]. I am enclosing a little collar which was made by a French lady in whose house we had our office and will send some more

---

70. Stanley refers to volunteers who received transfers to France from the 125th F. A. still training at Camp Cody.

little things like this pretty soon. Let me know if you get them alright. I received a letter from Mr. Fairchild at the Bank, one from Cousin Sidney and Uncle John and Aunt Emelia yesterday, have you heard from them lately, it seems as if they have changed their views on war considerably. Well I don't know of anything else to write so will close for this time; you hear more about the war than what we do so when you write tell me about it.

    With love to all I am
    Stanley
    Bn.Sgt.Maj.L.S.Williams, 151st F.A.
    [Censored by] O.K.. Everett F McCoy, 2 Lt 151 FA

★ ★ ★

                                        A.E.F. France
                                        July 3rd, 1918.

Mr. Alvin Williams:
    Request that the following articles be sent to me it approved.

        1 box cigars
        1 box candy, choclate bars
        1 dozen handkerchiefs

    L.S. Williams
    Bn. Sgt. Major, 151st Field Artillery
    A.E.F.
    Approved: Everett F. McCoy, 2nd Lt. 151st F.A.

Combat Operations, July 5–7

Two days prior to this letter, the 151st F. A. was placed in a defensive position on the Champagne front, combined with other units to blunt a heavy German assault. The Minnesota unit suffered the loss of 58 horses and one soldier killed in the first minutes of the attack. After several hours of deadly battle, a "great moment for the 151st" arrived—its artillery helped check the attack. Source: Collins, *History of the 151st Field Artillery*, 66–74, [quote 73].

AEF France
July 7, 1918

Dear Sister:

Will write you a few lines and let you know that I just recv'd your letter of June 9 and I am feeling fine as ever. Say about my allotment, let me know as soon as you can what one you recieved that is for what month etc. so that I can straighten it out. They are changed again now. so beginning with July I will not have an allotment but will send home by money order. Give a list of the checks by month that you recv'd. I am staying at the Echelon now and have the office here. and nothing to do.. I wrote a letter on the 3rd enclosing a collar, let me know if you get it. I guess Marland will not see France the way it looks now. and he is lucky. altho it is nice over [here] now, but war is war March all night and work all day sometimes we are almost like tramps now. would like to tell you where [shorthand symbol] I [shorthand symbol] am but cannot. If you here or know write and give the name [See the secret shorthand note below.]

Have you sold yet or are you going to stay where you are

Well I don't know of anything to write so will close for this time with love to all

Stanley

OK, Everett F McCoy, 2 Lt. [smudged] R 151 FA

Bn.Sgt.Maj.L.S.Williams, 151st FA

The shorthand symbols appear to be "champagne" and "front." Stan's Military Service Record confirms that he was present at Champagne-Marne, an offensive that spanned July 15 to 18, 1918, so in fact, he did find a way to communicate his location.

Under Attack

Determined to end the war in 1918, German military leaders launched a powerful series of coordinated attacks. The finale was the Champagne-Marne Offensive in July. The 42nd Rainbow Division, including its 151st Field Artillery, was among Allied units feeling the German fury. Col. George A. Leach, commander of the 151st, reported a "terrific" enemy bombardment "along a front of 100 kilometers [62 miles]" commencing at midnight on July 15.

Guns of the Minnesota unit and others along the Allied line boomed almost continually. The enemy made steady progress. Leach described the scene: "[Germans] have reached the intermediate [defensive] line and all our guns are going at top speed." While some forty German aircraft swooped down to machine-gun American positions, six huge tanks lumbered across trenches and through [barbed] wire. In response, at 8:40 a.m. the 42nd Division's infantry counterattacked and regained ground.[71]

Leach continued, "Noon and we have had four guns destroyed and a good many killed and wounded and it has been a perfect hell. Our [observation] balloon came down in

This Rainbow Division field dressing station was near Epieds, France. The wounded received treatment near battlefields before being moved to hospitals in the rear.

flames and both observers jumped safely." The colonel worried, "ammunition…is getting low." His artillery regiments would get little sleep in what proved to be a four-day battle. During brief respites, Leach's "tired artillery men would crawl under their blankets for a few moments sleep." Even under deadly enemy artillery fire, 151st artillerymen hauled food and ammunition to their field batteries. The Minnesota troops kept firing.

On July 16 the colonel noted that captured papers indicated the Germans had expected to move forward about ten miles. The Americans had yielded only two. "Terrific artillery fire all day and many air fights, with several balloons brought down," wrote Leach.

All along the line, Americans and their French comrades blunted the German assault. A French commander commended Col. Leach and his men, writing, their "spirit, coolness and gallantry have aroused universal admiration."

71. Here and below, "Monday July 15," in George E. Leach, *War Diary*, (Minneapolis: Pioneer Printers, 1923) 98–99. Colonel Leach led the 151st Field Artillery throughout the campaign in France. Leach was awarded a Croix de Guerre with palm for service in battle.

Combat Operations, July 18–August 3

Following its success in the July 15–18 victory over German forces, the 42nd Rainbow Division, and its 151st Field Artillery, moved northwest toward Chateau-Thierry. Stanley's letter below was written a week after their arrival. On July 26, the Rainbow Division, now attached to the 6th French Army, was pursuing retreating Germans. The next day they battled enemy troops dug in near the Ourcq River. Fighting continued for eight days when the German army was again forced back. Division losses were daunting. Upon its withdrawal from the line, 696 men had been killed, 4,240 wounded, and 578 were missing. Source: Collins, "Operations Report, July 25–August 3, 1918, 42nd Division," *History of the 151st Field Artillery*, 245–246.

AMERICAN YMCA
ON ACTIVE SERVICE
WITH THE
AMERICAN EXPEDITIONARY FORCES

July 30, 1918

Dear Folks:

Will write you a few lines and let you know I am still alive and feeling fine. I have received a couple of your letters lately

The reason that you do not get letters regularly is because we are on the move pretty much and mail does not go out, sometimes it is as much as a month so do not worry when you do not hear from me often. Things have been very exciting lately

Have not heard from Marland for a long time How is he, I suppose he will be on his way soon.

What does the papers over there say about the war. Do you think it will be over soon or not. It looks pretty good now I think.

Did you have a good time [on] the 4th: How is everybody down below. and say ask Uncle Ed. why he never answered my letter. I am going to write to a few of them pretty soon.

I wish Pa was here I would soon show him some things that would make his gardens and flowers look small. This country sure is pretty in the summer time and it certainly is shot up in some places too. If Marland was here he would have to get a few dozen extra pockets.

Well I do not know of anything to write so will close for this time with love to all

from Stanley

Bn.Sgt.Maj.L.S.Williams, 151 Field Art.

Send Back

Combat Operations, August 1918

On August 20, the 42nd Division was relieved by the 4th Division and recovering from its losses at the Ourcq and Vesle rivers. Two battalions of the 151st F. A. were temporarily attached to the 4th Division. Other Rainbow Division soldiers were enjoying a rest, including passes to Paris for some. Stanley was among them. Source: Collins, "Operations Report, July 25–August 3, 1918, 42nd Division," *History of the 151st Field Artillery*, 245–246.

Combat Operations, August-September, 1918

Stanley refers in the letter below to the September 1918 complaint issued by German officials through the Swiss government. The Germans protested the use of shotguns by American troops. They charged those weapons violated agreed-to regulations of war. Nearly 30,000 12-gauge Winchester Model 97 shotguns had been sent to U.S. infantry units. These rapid-fire weapons "fired a cloud of nine-buckshot with every shot." Known as trench sweepers or brooms, these weapons were used with devastating effect. Source: Thomas F. Swearengen, *The World's Fighting Shotguns*, (New York: T.B.N Enterprises, 1978) 10.

HEADQUARTERS SECOND BATTALION, 151ST F. A.

August 20th, 1918.

Dear Folks:

Will now write you a few lines again and let you know that I am still alive and feeling fine. We have been moving lately and are now in the S.O.S. [Services of Supply] which means back from the lines or in the rear and are back for a rest. We are located in a small town by the name of Daillecourt, about 30 kil. (20miles) East of Chaumont near Clefmont. I am also enclosing a copy of the Stars and Stripes which will tell you about what we have been doing and you will find a picture in their of a large German Gun Platform and I saw that so you can almost figure out where we have been and what we have been doing.

On the 15th 10 per cent of our regiment were given passes to Paris and I was there for 24 hours, the first time and I sure had the time of my life, Paris is almost the same as New York and it is almost like a real American place, I went down with about 300 Francs and came back broke, but then I bought a pair of high top lace boots which cost 140 francs and, I only hope I get another change to go there. I think we will soon get our 7 day passes altho nothing definite has been said yet. I made out another allotment commencing the first of August for $30.00 [$477] per month and let me know when you get it. When I wrote before I told you to let me [know] for which months you did not receive my allotment but as yet I have not heard from you. You should not receive any for the month of July.

Have not heard from Marland for quite a while, will he get a chance to come over here or not. I suppose he wants to come

American troops lean out of French railcars, as local citizens look on.

pretty bad. I sure have seen quite a bit of war lately and I am enclosing a lapel which I pulled off a dead Hun. [Soldiers of the 151st encountered more German dead in late August, including many unburied.] We handle them just like you would a dead dog, and as to using shot-guns as that piece in the paper says, why they use a few and if they don't I can't see why they shouldn't. A Hun will take advantage of you and so why shouldn't we do it, and we do not take more prisoners than necessary either.

Well I do not know of anything new to write about so will close for this time with love to all.

Stanley.

Bn.Sgt.Maj.L.S.Williams, 151st Field Artillery

[Censored by] Everett F McCoy, 2Lt___151FA

Combat Operations, September 9–15,1918

Field Order No. 17 was issued to the U.S. First Army. It detailed an assault against the St. Mihiel salient with 42nd Rainbow Division ordered to "attack in the center [of the German line] and deliver the main blow." The 151st Field Artillery was to provide artillery support to the 83rd and 84th Infantry Brigades. Source: Collins, *History of the 151st Field Artillery*, 255.

YMCA
ON ACTIVE SERVICE
WITH THE BRITISH EXPEDITIONARY FORCE

AEF France
Sept. 5, 1918

Dear Folks:

Will write you a few lines again and let you know I am still alive and everything is going good except It is raining today and it isn't very nice to be traveling and sleep outside. I am now in a British YMCA which accounts for this stationery.

I am sending you a couple copies of an order issued by our Division Commander and by that you can tell just what we have been doing and are going again. We have not had our 7 days leave yet and do not think that we will get them for a little while. The 24 hours I had in Paris is all the leave we have had and only a very few got them.

One of our Lt's Lieut Caldwell, whose home is in St. Paul left for home a week ago and I gave him your address and he said he would call you up. Let me know if he does. I think there will be some more going soon and one of them is coming over to see you

Have not heard from Marland for a long while.

Say My allotment was stopped for the mo's of July and Aug and will start with Sept for $30.00 [$477]. I put in a claim for the ones that you did not get. Well I will close for this time with love to all

Stanley

Bn Sgt Maj LS Williams,151 FA

General Charles Menoher, commander of the 42nd Division issued the
following laudatory summary of the unit's military operations to this time.

HEADQUARTERS, 42ND DIVISION
AMERICAN EXPEDITIONARY FORCES, FRANCE
AUGUST 13TH, 1918

TO THE OFFICERS AND MEN OF THE 42nd DIVISION:

A year has elapsed since the formation of your organization. It is, therefore, fitting to consider what you have accomplished as a combat division and what you should prepare to accomplish in the future.

Your first elements entered the trenches in Lorraine on February 21st. You served on that front for 110 days. You were the first American division to hold a divisional sector and when you left the sector June 21st, you had served continuously as a division in the trenches for a longer time than any other American division. Although you entered the sector without experience in actual warfare, you so conducted yourselves as to win the respect and affection of the French veterans with whom you fought. Under gas and bombardment, in raids, in patrols, in the heat of hand to hand combat and in the long dull hours of trench routine so trying to a soldier's spirit, you bore yourselves in a manner worthy of the traditions of our country.

You were withdrawn from Lorraine and moved immediately to the Champagne front where during the critical days from July 14th to July 18th, you had the honor of being the only American division to fight in General Gouraud's Army which so gloriously obeyed his order, "We will stand or die," and by its iron defense crushed the German assault and made possible the offensive of July 18th to the west of Reims.

From Champagne you were called to take part in exploiting the success north of the Marne. Fresh from the battle front before Chalons, you were thrown against the picked troops of Germany. For eight consecutive days, you attacked skillfully prepared positions. You captured great stores of arms and munitions. You forced crossings of the Ourcq. You took Hill 212, Sergy, Meurcy Ferme and Seringes by assault. You drove the enemy, including an Imperial Guard Division, before you for a depth of fifteen kilometers. When your infantry was relieved, it was in full pursuit of the retreating Germans, and your artillery continued to progress and support another American division in the advance to the Vesle.

For your services in Lorraine, your division was formally commended in General Orders by the French Army Corps under which you served. For your services in Champagne, your assembled officers received the personal thanks and commendation of General Gouraud himself. For your services on the Ourcq, your division was officially complimented in a letter from the Commanding General, 1st Army Corps, of July 28th, 1918.

To your success, all ranks and all services have contributed, and I desire to express to every man in the command my appreciation of his devoted and courageous effort.

However, our position places a burden of responsibility upon us which we must strive to bear steadily forward without faltering. To our comrades who have fallen, we owe the sacred obligation of maintaining the reputation which they died to establish. The influence of our performance on our allies and our enemies cannot be over-estimated for we were one of the first divisions sent from our country to France to show the world that Americans can fight.

Hard battles and long campaigns lie before us. Only by ceaseless vigilance and tireless preparation can we fit ourselves for them. I urge you, therefore, to approach the future with confidence but above all with firm determination that so far as it is in your power you will spare no effort whether in training or in combat to maintain the record of our division and the honor of our country.

CHARLES T. MENOHER,
Major General, U.S. Army

Combat Operations, September 12–15, 1918

An American assault began at 1 a.m. and made progress. "The Germans are leaving much behind and we captured whole [artillery] batteries complete…. About 10,000 prisoners to date." As the attackers moved forward, large stores of enemy equipment and food were captured. The Rainbow Division advanced about 12 miles while relying on German rations. 42nd Division losses: 139 killed, 628 wounded, 35 missing. Source: Collins, "Report on Operations of the 42nd Division, September 11 to September 15…St. Mihiel Salient," *History of the 151st Field Artillery*, 266–270.

A.E.F. France
Sept. 19th, 1918.

Dear Folks:

Will write you a few lines and let you know that I am still alive and feeling fine. Received three of your letters yesterday and, say I thot that you were thru moving and were going to stay on one place long enough to find out what it was like. I suppose by the time I get home you will be out in the country again and wishing you were back where you started from.

Everything is going fine and if you will read the papers you can judge for yourself what is going on. At present I have my office in a place that the Boche used about a week ago. Saw some Red Wing boys that were sent over as Casuals from the 125th and Ted Peterson is with them. They all knew Marland well. I suppose he is still at Fort Sill.

I am enclosing an order and I think that this one will work all right. You can use my allotment money for anything you wish, it don't amount to much but I guess I will have enough to buy some clothes when the guerre [war] is over. Received a letter from Sidney [Peterson] yesterday also and I see that they have changed their views as regards to what is going on. Hoping this will find you all O.K. I will close for this time with love to all, from
Stanley.

Combat Operations, September 26–October 8, 1918

The Meuse–Argonne Offensive, "the war's largest combined [U.S.-French] movement," opened with a brigade of the 151st F. A. in action. By October 5, they "were in the thick of fighting," working with the 72nd and 32nd divisions (the 42nd was in reserve) on the drive for Montfaucon. The 42nd returned to action on October 10, with six batteries of the 151st F. A. in support. German units were in a slow retreat. Source: *Northwest Warriors*, 60. Collins, "Report on Operations of the 42nd Division, September 11 to September 15… St. Mihiel Salient," *History of the 151st Field Artillery*, 271–282.

[Envelope addressed to Mr. Alvin Williams, 391 Arundel St., St. Paul, Minnesota, U.S.A. Return address: Bn Sgt Maj LS Williams, FA.]

YMCA
ON ACTIVE SERVICE
WITH THE
AMERICAN EXPEDITIONARY FORCES

Oct 15, 1918

Dear Folks

Will write you a few lines again and let you know everything is still OK and that we are still at it but in a different place. I am going to send you a Boche helmet as soon as we get back a ways. Recv'd a couple of your letters a few days ago and also one from a Miss Eldrdge of Brainerd. She said you gave her my address but as yet I have not ans. her and maybe won't.

Say, you won't me to write to different people at home, but I can't see why they can't write to me first just as well If some of them can't write I do not see why I should, or how?

I am enclosing a Xmas coupon which you can fill if you wish. Please enclose a wristwatch (Ingersoll) as I have none and French watches are <u>par bon</u> [no good][72]

I have not heard from Marland yet but expect that if he is over here that I will soon.

In regard to that lot that you mentioned in your letter you can take my allotment money and use for it or whatever you think best.

Well there is no news around here to send except that the guns are making a lot of noise and a few Boshe shells coming in at times so will close with love to all

Stanley.

Combat Operations, October 31–November 2, 1918

The 151st reached the line at Grand Pre Brieulles on the banks of the Meuse near Sedan. Charles Summerall, commanding general, issued a formal commendation to all 5th Army Corps artillery units, including Stanley's 151st Field Artillery. They had been "constantly in action day and night…since the beginning of the present offensive." The 42nd and its artillery arm had been temporarily transferred to the 5th Army. Losses in the 42nd Division from October 10 to November 8: 395 killed, 632 severely wounded, 721 gassed, 91 missing. Sources: Collins, *History of the 151st Field Artillery*, 298–299, 309–311, *Northwest Warriors*, 60.

72. Wristwatches came into use around 1916 because pocket watches proved to be difficult for soldiers to access quickly and inconspicuously. Many wristwatches had radium numbers for viewing in the dark.

France,
Oct. 24th, 1918.

Dear Folks:

Will write a few lines again today and let you know that I am still alive and feeling fine except for a little cold, and kicking about the mud. At present I am living on a hillside where two other fellows and myself dug a hole in the side of the hill to make it level to sleep on and we have a 12 x 12 tarp stretched over it which makes a fairly good home and better than most of them have it. But the mud is worse of all as it rains 3 out of 4 days and take where an advance has been made and the roads are all tore up and new ones made, and also where they drive into places used as echelons it gets so bad that they sometimes get stuck with an empty wagon. But then so long as everything is going so good, and I suppose you know more about it than we do, that we do not mind it so much, but at that the war cannot end too soon, we have two service strips [stripes] now and I sure do hope that it is over before we can get a third.

Say is Marland over here yet or not, have not heard a word from him for a long time. If he is I do not think that they will be on the front for a while as they generally have to go thru a training camp first.

I recv'd a couple of your letters the other day and in regard to what you said about writing I wish that you would write a couple every day as a letter from home is the best thing that I could wish for. When I get back to the S.O.S. where I can get to buy something, I will send it to the girls. I sent you a Xmas package coupon about a week ago and asked for a wrist watch, so if you can send me an Ingersoll; an ingersoll lasts longer than the best French watch you can buy. I am going to send you a couple of German helmets in a few days if I can get them thru but it is pretty hard to send anything now. Well I will have to close now so with love to all I will quit with love to all

Stanley
Bn.Sgt.Maj. L.S.Williams
151st Field Artillery.
"OK, BM Randall

War Deaths

It is difficult to comprehend the cost in lives of the Great War. While exact numbers cannot be determined, accurate estimates have been made. Historian John Keagan assembled evidence about the losses to the French and German armies that fought from the war's first day, July 28, 1914, to the last, November 11, 1918. Of France's roughly ten million men of military age, 300,000 were killed and 600,000 wounded in the first four months of fighting.

By Armistice Day 1918, nearly two million Frenchmen had been killed and some five million wounded. By the war's end, fighting decreased the number of German men aged 19 to 22 by 35 to 37 percent. Thirteen percent of Germany's 16 million men born between 1870 and 1899 died in the war—a death rate of 465,000 per year. Germany's final toll was 2.1 million soldiers dead.

All totaled, the Allies—France and its colonies, Great Britain and the British Empire, smaller allied nations, and the United States—sustained 5.6 million war deaths. The empires of Germany, Austria-Hungary, Ottoman Turks and Bulgaria had 4.4 million killed. American dead from all causes numbered 116,700. Sources: John Keagan, *The First World War* (New York: Alfred A. Knopf, 1999) 5–7. Antoine Prost, "War Losses," International Encyclopedia of the First World War, http://encyclopedia.1914-1918-online.net/article/war_losses. The author offers explanatory comments regarding how casualty totals were analyzed and reported.

On the firing line in the Great War

Army of Occupation Operations, November 16, 1918

The 151st Field Artillery began moving toward the Rhine River on November 16. A part of the U.S. Army of Occupation, the 42nd Rainbow Division was one of six to be assigned to take control of German territory. The 151st reached Heimersheim, Germany, about 18 miles northwest of Koblenz, on December 15. The 42nd garrisoned 21 of the 122 towns in their area of supervision. Source: Collins, *History of the 151st Field Artillery*, 313–314.

Headquarters Second Battalion 151ST F. A.

November 19th, 1918.

Dear Folks:

Will write you a few lines again and let you know that I am still alive and things are going pretty fine. Now that that war is over everybody is waiting for the day that we can go home, and taking into consideration the fact that we are among the first over here and have done about as much fighting as any American Division I think that we will be some of the first to go Home.

I have received two letters from Marland since he got over here but I have not seen him and doubt that I will unless we happen to pass them sometime while on the march. We are now headed for Germany as I understand we are to be part of the Army of Occupation. One of the rumors that is going around is that we will go in as an army of occupation and after Armistice is over we will go right home.

I suppose the people in the States are having some great times now, and we would too but the Germans have retreated so far and we are in that area where there are no civilians and everything is shot up, and it don't hardly seem any different now than before it was over except that there is no firing etc. You can talk about camping out but when you march all day and halt after dark on a hill side this time of the year where there is no shelter and almost zero whether, the end of the war cannot be appreciated enough. When some of these S.O.S. birds get home and tell about the nice places they had etc. and I am around somebody is going to have a sore head.

Well I do not know of much to write so hoping that I can be home soon and everything is over I will close with love to all
Stanley.
O.K., H.H. Scott, 1st Lt., 151 F.A. A.E.F.

★ ★ ★

Heimersheim, Germany
December 17th, 1918.

Dear Folks:

Will write you a few lines in answer to five of yours which I received yesterday, dated from Oct. 21st to Nov. 11th. We Arrived at this place day before yesterday and expect to stay here for quite a while as this is supposed to be our destination while a part of the Army of Occupation. We are almost 30 Kilometers [about 19 miles] north of Coblenz and about 5 kil. from the Rhine. This is some country, nothing but hills, almost mountains, and around where we are now everything is covered with vineyards. The people seem to be pretty well to do and as far as I can see the German people are not as bad off as they say, that is in the small places but I guess it is different in the big cities. Some of them treat us pretty good and even if they do not want to give what we are supposed to get, we take it anyway. Most of them think it is funny because we ask and pay for what we get, but the Germans would help themselves and do to the German people just about what they did to the Belgiums and French, but they all say that they are glad it is the Americans that are coming thru and not the French.[73]

Have not heard from Marland since about the 1st of November wonder if his outfit has been sent back or not, we are so far from France now that I do not think I will ever see it again. It sure was some hike but now that it is over why things seem pretty good again, I have an office in a private house and in the room is an electric light, stove and best of all a good BED, altho I have been sleeping in beds for about the last two weeks But at that the day cannot come to soon when I can come home to you, whether it be in St. Paul or out in the country, Have you bought that place yet or not.

73. Those living in Germany's large cities suffered more than most residents of self-sufficient rural areas. The economy was in shambles, unemployment was high, violent struggles for political power were underway and shortages of food and power were becoming more frequent. For an overview of this crisis in the immediate aftermath of the war see Anthony Read, *The World on Fire: 1919 and the Battle with Bolshevism* (New York: W. W. Norton, 2008) 44–50, 66–78.

Say you said in one of your letters that this fellow Danielson[74] was getting in trouble and that he had a Croix de Guerre etc.[75] Well I know him pretty well and a whole lot better than you do and a little while in the cop [coop] wouldn't hurt him a bit, and as far as bravery is concerned all those that got cited at that time, was because they happened to be the first Americans wounded, so when all these fellows that are good talkers come to your meetings and began telling about this and that, think twice before you say anything. That fellow I was telling you about is one of the boys that was in this detail, he was supposed to go home but after I wrote that letter the order was changed and he is still here so you see you are all wrong in supposing what you did.

Well I will close for this time and will write oftener now so with love to all I remain

Stanley

O.K., H.H. Scott, 1st Lt. 151 F.A.

Heimersheim, Germany
26 December 1918

Dear Folks:

Will write a few more lines again and let you know I am still in Germany. Xmas is now over but wish that I could of spent it at home instead of over here. We had quite a dinner yesterday and in the afternoon we rode down to the Rhine river which is only about 8 kil. from this town.

I received both the Xmas package and the other one a couple of days before Xmas and they certainly were great, but the watch was best of all. I hope I can get lots of money so I can make good use of that belt. I just said the watch was best but after eating that cake I think I will have to change it. The last letter I received from you

74. Stanley refers to Pvt. Charles Danielson who was among five members of the 151st F. A. to be wounded in a March 5, 1917, artillery attack. They were the regiment's first casualties. Sgt. Theodor Petersen, among the five, died of wounds following the attack, and received the French *Croix de Guerre* and the U.S. Distinguished Service Cross. The regiment's history notes twenty-seven soldiers received the French award, but does not name them. Collins, *History of the 151st Field Artillery, 39–40, 407*.

75. The *Croix de Guerre* (war cross) is a French military decoration awarded to French and allied soldiers for feats of bravery. "Chemins de Memoire," http://www.cheminsdememoire.gouv.fr/en/la-croix-de-guerre.

was dated the 11 of November the day the Armistice started. And I have not heard from Marland for quite a while, I am beginning to think that He may be on his way home by this time. According to rumors, of which there are always plenty, we will be starting for home in about a month and that time cannot come too soon to suit me. I suppose some of the boys that were over here are already back now.

I am enclosing a few cards which will give you and idea of how some of the places around here look. I would have sent home some souviners but we have not been able to send any second class mail and when we entered Germany we were not supposed to have anything that was German on us, but at that I have an Iron Cross and a couple "Got Mit Uns" [God with us] Buckles etc. which I will take with me when I come home. Well I do not know of anything else to write about so will close with love to all

Stanley.

★ ★ ★

Heimersheim, Germany,
Jan. 15th, 1919.

Dear Folks:

I have just received three of your letters, Dec. 16, 18 and and 25th and one from Marland written on New Year's Eve. He said that he had had the influ[76]. and pneumonia and was not able to go back with the regiment, missing it by a couple of hours, but I suppose he is on his way now with one of the Casual Companies (wish I was in his Shoes) I do not expect that we will get home for at least 3 or 4 months April at the earliest Things here are about the same every day, drill etc. The German people here treat us pretty good but they cannot see where the ways of the German Army was wrong and lots of them still stick up for the Kaiser. They have plenty to eat, but I guess in the big cities it is not so good.

Say will you send me a list next time you write of the number of allotment checks or amount of allotment money you have got so

---

76. The devastating influenza pandemic of 1918–1919 was underway. About half of the U.S. soldiers who died in Europe were killed by flu. "The Influenza Pandemic of 1918," https://virus.stanford.edu/uda/.

I can check up and see that it is straight. I want to do this before we go back so that It will be O.K. when we get discharged. I notice when you write you address my mail to the Battery, but I am not even with the Battery as I now belong to Headquarters Company and am with the 2nd Bn. Hq., Battery "C" being in the 1st Bn. So after this when you write only put Hq. Company, 151st F.A. You say the Rainbow Division has a high standing and that everybody is talking about it, but if they think so much of us, WHY DON'T THEY DO SOMETHING TO GET US HOME SOON.

I suppose it is pretty cold now and lots of snow, here I have only seen snow once and it hasn't been any colder than what the people can work in the field, plow etc. It seems quite strange to see the way they do things, and they use oxen mostly, horses being pretty scarce. Have you got a new place yet, I bet you will never get a place that will satisfy you more than a year or two-------I am sending that order and do not be afraid to use it. Well I do not know of anything else to write so will close for this time with love to all.

Stanley.

Government-supplied postcards informed families of a soldier's location, organization and condition of health.

Heimersheim, Germany
9 February 1919.

Dear Folks:

Will now write you a few lines again and hope this will find you all well and hope that none of you will have the flu anymore. I suppose Marland is home by this time, or that you have [at] least heard from him. The last letter I recv'd from him was written on New Year's Eve and he told me about having the flu and pneumonia but was ready then to start for home.

I am feeling fine now but I did have a bad cold for a couple of days and also a tooth that gave me some trouble, it ached for two or three days and the dentist could do nothing to stop it, so he pulled it and it had started an abscess, it was one of the back teeth so it didn't make much difference.

We are still in the same place and do not as yet know when we will leave but there is always lots of rumors and according to them, we will leave here the first of March but I doubt it, every week that we have to stay here seems almost like a year and I sure will be glad when we get started on our way. It has been about 0 weather the last couple of days and a little patch of snow here and there and this is about the only cold weather we have had. The men have to drill every day and then they have the horses to take care of but at that the men in the Army of Occupation have it better than the men stationed in France.

A week ago tomorrow they gave about 2000 men from this Div a pass to Coblenz and I got one of them, it was only for a day but I had a pretty good time at that. They are giving passes to different places around here quite often now. The Corp. I have working in the office with me went on a fourteen day pass to different places in France yesterday. When he gets back I am going, I will go thru Paris to Lyon, Toulouse and some other places. I cannot get a pass to Sweden or I would go there.

How do you like your new place, I think you would be better off on a small place out around the lakes, but then if you get tired of it I guess you can easily make the change. What is Marland going to do. Will he have a chance to keep on with his music or not. I see Illinois is going to give their solders a 6 months bonus, what is

Minnesota going to do, nothing I suppose. They showed the Mile of Smiles here about a week ago and I saw you in it but It went so fast that a glimpse was all I got.

Well everything is going the same, so I will close with love to all hoping that I will be home to see you within the next six months [77]
Stanley

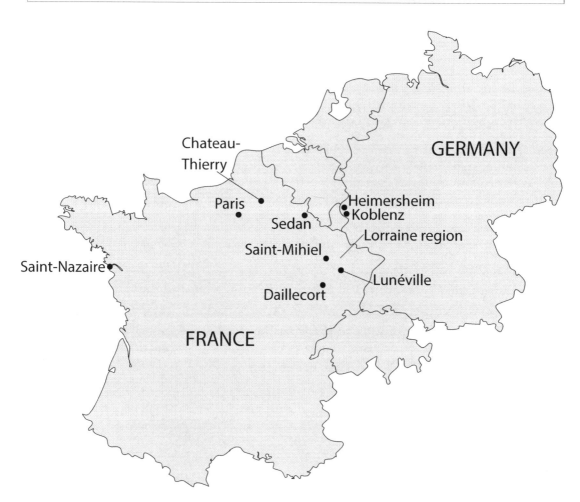

Places significant to the 151st F. A.: Saint-Nazaire, the port at which it landed; the Lorraine region where they first underwent combat; Chateau-Thierry 56 miles north of Paris and Saint-Mihiel, in the province of Champagne, sites of two famed and costly battles; and Heimersheim, Germany, where it served in the peacetime Army of Occupation.

77. Stanley's hope to return to Minnesota was fulfilled on March 22, when this order arrived: "General Orders No. 20. Pursuant to telegraphic instructions from General Headquarters…the 42nd Division on March 22, 1919, was relieved from duty with the Third Army…and placed under the orders of the Commanding General, S.O.S. for preparation for shipment to port…for embarkation to the United States.—By Command of Major General Flagler" *Collins*, History of the 151st Field Artillery, 325.

Forwarded 5/11/20. Approved by H.R.Packard Capt Inf
for Victory Medal with Clasps.

ENLISTMENT RECORD.

Name: Stanley L. Williams Grade: Sergeant Major,

Enlisted, or Inducted, April 23, 1917, at St Paul, Minn

Serving in First enlistment period at date of discharge.

Prior service: * None

Noncommissioned officer: Sgt Major R 3028, April 6 1918.

Marksmanship, gunner qualification or rating: † Not Rated.

Horsemanship: Not Mounted.

Battles, engagements, skirmishes, expeditions: A E F Born with Champagne, Marne, St Mihiel Offen Muse Argonne Sectors,

DECORATIONS: MEDALS: BADGES: Citation: None,

Knowledge of any vocation: Clerk,

Wounds received in service: None

Physical condition when discharged: Good

Typhoid prophylaxis completed: Sept 17

Paratyphoid prophylaxis completed:

Married or single: Single

Character: Excellent

Remarks: No A W O L No absences under G O 31 & GO 45 1917 Entitled to travel pay Left U.S. Act 18 1917 Arrived U.S. April 26 1919.

Signature of soldier: L Stanley Williams

CAMP DODGE, IOWA
MAY 10 1919
Paid in Full Including
Bonus $108.03
A. A. Padmore
Capt. Quartermaster, U.S.A.

Commanding

*Give company and regiment or corps or department, with inclusive dates of service in each enlistment.
†Give date of qualification or rating and number, date, and source of order announcing same.

Honorable Discharge from The United States Army

TO ALL WHOM IT MAY CONCERN:

This is to Certify, That* *Stanley L. Williams*

†*1,43,675 Sgt Major. Casual Det. 411— 163 DB*
(Last assigned Btry C 151 FA.)

THE UNITED STATES ARMY, *as a* TESTIMONIAL OF HONEST AND FAITHFUL

SERVICE, *is hereby* HONORABLY DISCHARGED *from the military service of the*

UNITED STATES *by reason of* ‡ *Tel WD MD 15/18 Tra 4a Nov 30/18.*

Said *Stanley L. Williams* *was born*

in *Hager City*, *in the State of* *Wisconsin*

When enlisted he was *21¾* *years of age and by occupation a* *Clerk.*

He had *blue* *eyes,* *brown* *hair,* *fair* *complexion, and*

was *6* *feet* *0* *inches in height.*

Given under my hand at *Camp Dodge Iowa* *this*

10 *day of* *May*, *one thousand nine hundred and* *Nineteen*

True copy made by me Oct 7-1519 for the
purpose of securing soldiers Bonus granted
under chapt 49 Extra Legislative Session 1519
State of Minnesota

Louis Cearnal

Major Signal Corps USA

Commanding.

A Van Slyke

NOTARY PUBLIC, Ramsey Co., Minn.
My Commission expires May 8, 1921.

Form No. 525, A. G. O.   *Insert name, Christian name first; e. g., "John Doe."
Oct. 9-18.   †Insert Army serial number, grade, company and regiment or arm or corps or department; e. g., "1,620,302"; "Corporal,
   Company A, 1st Infantry"; "Sergeant, Quartermaster Corps"; "Sergeant, First Class, Medical Department."
2—3164   ‡If discharged prior to expiration of service, give number, date, and source of order or full description of authority therefor.

Photographs

Barber Shop

Ball Headed Bunch

Supply Wagons

Dad the News Boy

Bat. B Corral

Shoeing a Bad One

Some Hoss

Breaking Him

Prize Fight

Football

In Concealment

Big Rock

Holding On

Sights on Our Trip

Taking a Rest

On the Mountain

Going Up

Soldiers on a Mine Car

Off for a Ride

Sights on Our Trip

Silver Mines

Mountains in New Mexico

A Three Inch

Making Streets

Marland Williams

Xmas Dinner

Power House Copper Mine

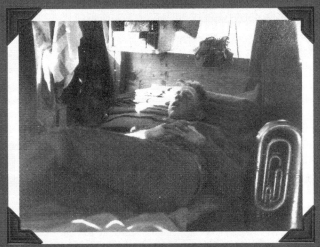

Taking a Nap

Band

Our Street

Our Camp

Cleaning Up

Tenting in the Desert

Our Squad

Scrapbook

Marland Williams worked at the YMCA in Red Wing while he attended Red Wing Seminary, ca. 1915.

National Guard drilling near Duluth (Minnesota) Curling Club

Red Wing Seminary Band: Stanley, holding his saxophone, third row, third from left; Marland holding his cornet, same row, far right.

Thanksgiving Dinner
November 29, 1917

Headquarters Co.
125th FIELD ARTILLERY
Camp Cody, New Mexico

HISTORY OF HEADQUARTERS COMPANY
125th FIELD ARTILLERY.

Called into service July 15th, 1917, at Duluth, Minnesota. Mustered in August 5th, 1917. Strength of Company at that time was one officer and 58 enlisted men. Captain W. O. Flodin was in command of the Company, which was then a part of the 3rd Minn. Infantry.

Company left Duluth August 27th, 1917, and arrived at Camp Cody, Deming, New Mexico, August 31st. The Company took up active training as an infantry organization and remain such until October 1st when we were transferred to the Artillery and made into the Headquarters Company of the 125th Field.

We now have 14 officers and 166 enlisted men in the Company. The company is composed of the old headquarters Company, a part of what used to be K Company of the 3rd Minnesota and also some men were transferred from old B Company and a few from some of the other companies.

Menu
———

Cream of Tomato Soup

Olives   Sweet Gherkins   Celery

Roast Young Turkey

Cranberry Sauce   Oyster Dressing

Mashed Potatoes

Sliced Ripe Tomatoes   Green Peas

Coffee   Cocoa

Bread   Butter

Mince Pie   Pumpkin Pie

Vanity Wafers   Vanilla Wafers

Mixed Nuts   Assorted Fruits

Cigars
and
Cigarettes

Roster
Headquarters Company, 125th F. A.

Captain Chester S. Wilson
1st Lieutenant Edward B. Cutter
1st Lieutenant Rudolf Gaalaas
1st Lieutenant Eugene C. Kalkman
1st Lieutenant J. J. Lieb
1st Lieutenant Earl E. Marsh
1st Lieutenant Daniel McDonald
1st Lieutenant John W. Signer
2nd Lieutenant Purcell E. Barker
2nd Lieutenant Carl Haglund
2nd Lieutenant Lynn C. Kelly
2nd Lieutenant Edwin F. Postal
2nd Lieutenant William C. Risse
2nd Lieutenant A. M. Watkins

REG. SGT. MAJOR
Pease, John G.

BN. SGT. MAJOR
Laux, Paul V.
Haroldson, Harry

COLOR SERGEANTS
Smith, Justin V.
Wright, Thomas H. C.

1st SGT. AND DRUM MAJOR
McCarthy, John E.

MESS SERGEANT
Anderson, Arthur A.

SUPPLY SERGEANT
Nixon, Joseph E.

STABLE SERGEANT
Donne, William R.

SERGEANTS
Berg, Henry W.
Bourdaghs, Clarence D.
Carlisle, Lloyd W.
Caswell, Arthur D.
Douglass, Robert M.
Enewold, David A.
Foster, Charles I.
Fryklund, Vern C.
Libby, Burt P.
Moe, James J.
West, Frank

CORPORALS
Bussingwhite, Sterling R.
Bessonen, Beuhart B.
Bowers, Warren C.
Bradshaw, Clifford W.
Braton, Merritt
Brekken, Willie H.
Dirimple, Kenneth
Finnemore, James
Finnemore, Harold
Forcien, George F.
Holan, John G.
Holter, Alvin C.
Grove, Ray C.
Heiserman, Charles W.
Kidd, James W.
Martin, Leville F.
McCarthy, Leo M.
Merrill, James H.
Powerlet, Frank H.
Roberts, Roy C.
Schefefine, Gustav C.
Sherman, Merritt R.
Sturr, Clifford G.
Smith, Henry M.
Thorburn, John R.
Van Prang, Harry
Wethern, Milton E.
Wethern, Rudolph J.
Wyberg, Victor R.

Roster—[Continued]
——————

SADDLER
Loftus, Stephen T.

HOUSESHOERS
Campbell, Alan G.
Sawyer, Clarence H.

MECHANICS
Ekstrom, George C.
Ogren, John R.

BUGLERS
Chase, Charles W.
Groven, Gerhard
Hamlin, John H.

COOKS
Ryan, George O.
Collopy, Frank J.
Tracy, Edmund

BAND SECTION

Band Leader
Grimm, Alfred

Asst. Band Leader
White, Louis W.

Sgt. Bugler
Grimm, Robert G.

Band Sergeants
Rousquet, Arthur J.
McDougall, Anthony G.

Band Corporals
Chalman, Arthur H.
Parker, Raymond E.
Anderson, Roland C.
Smith, Melbourne

Musicians 1st Class
Hentges, John W.
Slipka, Frank E.

Musicians 2nd Class
Casola, Henry
Erickson, John M.
Pope, Richard J.

Musicians 3rd Class
Andlag, Charles
De Bernhardi, Angelo
Johnson, Raymond
Larson, Halfdau C.
Lindseth, Clarence A.
Moran, John J.
McMahan, Albert J.
Newton, Clair L.
O'Grady, Matt F.
Porter, Sherman C.
Ramstad, Sigurd S.
Schaefer, Alvin C.
Williams, Marland R.

PRIVATES 1st CLASS

Anderson, Arthur E.
Aske, Charles
Bernard, John F.
Bunker, Theodore
Burke, Clarence T.
Brewer, Charles
Brexler, William T.
Campbell, Frank W.
Clayton, Lawrence H.
Feda, Frank M.
Hauger, Jacob
Johnson, Bert E.
Kelleher, Robert F.
Killin, Russell
Larson, Oscar E.
Lome, William J.
McCarthy, Daniel T.
Nelson, Arthur A.
Nordeen, Paul L.
Postal, Robert
Pratt, Robert G.
Richardson, Donald R.
Scott, Lawrence H.
Sharp, Harold H.
Silker, Rollin C.

Roster—[Continued]
——————

PRIVATES

Barthe, Edmund L.
Berglund, Alvin
Besnet, John L.
Bille, Henry
Bjorlin, Victor L.
Bradfield, Clarence F.
Broecker, Harold F.
Carroll, Charlie B.
Carlson, Edward C.
Chinander, Erwin A.
Christensen, Irving P.
Day, John
De Mars, Leon M.
Dunn, Lawrence A.
Engstrom, Reynold E.
Florine, Frank B.
George, George T.
Giebler, George E.
Gilmont, Lawrence L.
Guertin, Louis
Hammar, Emil F.
Hauck, Walter A.
Heinecke, Percy E.
Heisterkamp, Henry R.
Hughes, John A.
Hust, Erwin J.
Kappel, Nicholas
Leonard, Arthur V.
Lindell, Walter L.
Lynch, Patrick E.
Lynch, James E.
Lund, Elmer A.
Mark, Olaf H.
McDonnell, James G.
McGraw, Fred
McNeal, Leon
Miller, Floyd D.
Moisan, Max
Murray, John H.
Osmundson, Martin
Pontnville, Eugene
Pusch, Adolph
Rosenquist, Emmet C.
Skramstad, Arthur I.
Salmoiraghi, Paul C.
Stearns, Clyde C.
Taylor, Archie
Thomas, Chester V.
Thompson, Harold N.
Thompson, George E.
Van Elsberg, Robert J.
Whalen, George H.
White, Frank H.

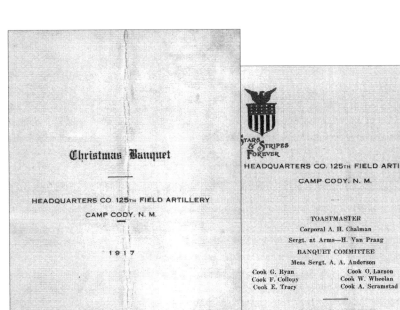
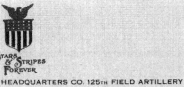

Christmas Banquet

HEADQUARTERS CO. 125TH FIELD ARTILLERY

CAMP CODY. N. M.

1917

STARS & STRIPES FOREVER

HEADQUARTERS CO. 125TH FIELD ARTILLERY

CAMP CODY. N. M.

TOASTMASTER

Corporal A. H. Chalman

Sergt. at Arms—H. Van Praag

BANQUET COMMITTEE

Mess Sergt. A. A. Anderson

Cook G. Ryan	Cook O. Larson
Cook F. Collopy	Cook W. Wheelan
Cook E. Tracy	Cook A. Scramstad

RECEPTION COMMITTEE

Sergt. Douglas, Chairman	Corp. H. Smith
Corp. Anderson	Corp. McCarthy
Corp. Chalman	

ORCHESTRA

Oscar Erickson, Leader--	Violin
John Moran	Cornet
Frank Slipka	Trombone
Arthur Bosquet	Clarinet
Angelo Di Bernardi	Flute
J. Erickson	Drums, Traps, Xylophone
John Hamlin	Guitar

MENU

Olives	Sweet Gherkins	Celery

Roast Young Turkey

Cranberry Sauce	Oyster Dressing

Mashed Potatoes

Sliced Ripe Tomatoes	Green Peas

Grape Frappe

White Bread and Butter

Apple Pie	Currant Pie
Vanity Wafers	Vanilla Wafers
Mixed Nuts	Assorted Fruits

Cigars

PROGRAM

Orchestra .... Selection

125th Field Artillery March

(Dedicated to Band Leader Grimm. Composed by Oscar R. Erickson, 125th F. A. Band.)

Address .... Why We Celebate Christmas

Chaplain Ralmshaw

Vocal Solo .... Joy to the World

Corporal Anderson

Violin Solo .... Selected

Miss Jean Smith

Cornet Solo .... "Somewhere"

Band Leader Grimm

Guitar Solo .... "Gravy" (Nonsense)

Reynold Engstrom

Orchestra .... Selection

Wedding of Roses.

Reading .... School of a Soldier (By Brainless Bates)

Henry Smith

Xylophone Solo .... Weaving Around

John Erickson

Vocal Solo .... "Somewhere a Voice Is Calling"

John Bernard

Orchestra .... Selection

Sweet Emiline, My Gal

Strutters Quartet ....

Sgt. Berg, Carlisle, Douglas and Bugler Chase

Poem .... Face on the Barroom Floor

Lieutenant Postal

Xylophone Violin Duet .... "Perfect Day"

(By Request. By Erickson Brothers)

Address .... Reminiscences from the French Front

By Sergeant Dumont of the French Artillery

Address .... Captain Wilson

Vocal Solo .... "Marseilaise"

(By Request. By John Bernard)

America ....

By Audience

Star Spangled Banner ....

Exit March .... Strutters' Ball

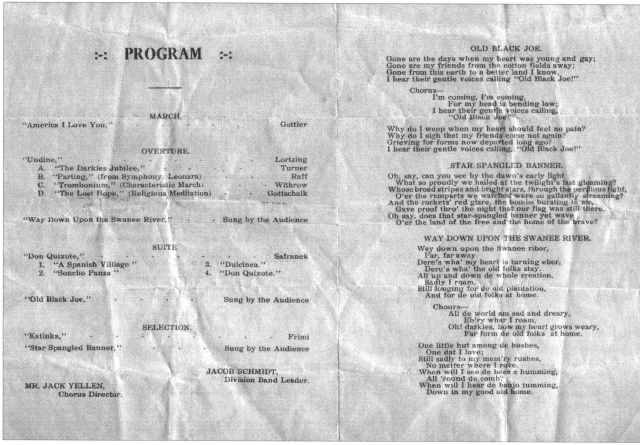

:-: PROGRAM :-:

MARCH.
"America I Love You,"   Gottler

OVERTURE.
"Undine,"   Lortzing
A. "The Darkies Jubilee,"   Turner
B. "Parting," (from Symphony: Leonara)   Raff
C. "Trombonium," (Characteristic March)   Withrow
D. "The Lost Hope," (Religious Meditation)   Gottschalk

"Way Down Upon the Swanee River,"   Sung by the Audience

SUITE
"Don Quixote,"   Safranek
1. "A Spanish Villiage."   3. "Dulcinea."
2. "Soncho Panza "   4. "Don Quixote."

"Old Black Joe,"   Sung by the Audience

SELECTION.
"Katinka,"   Frimi
"Star Spangled Banner,"   Sung by the Audience

JACOB SCHMIDT,
Division Band Leader.

MR. JACK YELLEN,
Chorus Director.

OLD BLACK JOE.
Gone are the days when my heart was young and gay;
Gone are my friends from the cotton fields away;
Gone from this earth to a better land I know,
I hear their gentle voices calling "Old Black Joe!"

Chorus—
I'm coming, I'm coming,
For my head is bending low;
I hear their gentle voices calling,
"Old Black Joe!"

Why do I weep when my heart should feel no pain?
Why do I sigh that my friends come not again?
Grieving for forms now departed long ago?
I hear their gentle voices calling, "Old Black Joe!"

STAR SPANGLED BANNER.
Oh, say, can you see by the dawn's early light
What so proudly we hailed at the twilight's last gleaming?
Whose broad stripes and bright stars, through the perilous fight,
O'er the ramparts we watched were so gallantly streaming?
And the rockets' red glare, the bombs bursting in air,
Gave proof thro' the night that our flag was still there.
Oh, say, does that star-spangled banner yet wave
O'er the land of the free and the home of the brave?

WAY DOWN UPON THE SWANEE RIVER.
Way down upon the Swanee ribor,
Far, far away.
Dere's wha' my heart is turning eber,
Dere's wha' the old folks stay.
All up and down de whole creation,
Sadly I roam.
Still longing for de old plantation,
And for de old folks at home.

Chours—
All de world am sad and dreary,
Eb'ry whar I roam,
Oh! darkies, how my heart grows weary,
Far form de old folks at home.

One little hut among de bushes,
One dat I love;
Still sadly to my mem'ry rushes,
No matter where I rove.
When will I see de bees a humming,
All 'round de comb?
When will I hear de banjo tumming,
Down in my good old home.

Program from March 3, 1918

Headquarters Co., Second Battalion, 151st F. A., 42nd Rainbow Division

PROGRAM

———

March, "Columbia"..Lewis

Overture, "The Queen Secret"..............................Amb. Thomas

a. Listen to that Dixie Band......................Yellen & Cobb

b. Intermezzo   Agnus Dei....................................Bizet

c. Waltz   The Skater...............................Waldteufel

Song......................................."Keep the Home Fires Burning"
(Sung by the Audience)

Selection, "I Lombardi"..Verdi

Fantasia. "A Spanish Festival"...........................Demersseman

Arrival of Guests..The Hunt

The Bolero...Spanish Hymn

"Star Spangled Banner"...........................(Sung by the Audience)

MR. JACK YELLEN,   JACOB SCHMIDT,
    Chorus Director.   Division Band Leader.

"KEEP THE HOME FIRES BURNING."

I.

They were summoned from the hillside,
    They were called in from the glen,
And the country found them ready
    At the stirring call for men.
Let no tears add to their hardships:
    As the soldiers march along,
Even tho your heart is breaking
    Make it sing this cheery song:

CHORUS.

Keep the Home Fires burning,
While your hearts are yearning,
Though your lads are far away.
They dream of home.
There's a silver lining
Through the dark clouds shining,
Turn the dark clouds inside out
Till the boys come home.

"STAR SPANGLED BANNER."

Oh, thus be it ever when freeman shall stand
Between their loved homes and the war's desolation
Blest with victory and peace, may the heav'n-rescued land
Praise the Pow'r that hath made and preserved us a nation.
Then conquer we must, when our cause it is just,
And this be our motto : "In God is our trust !"
And the Star Spangled Banner in triumph shall wave
O'er the land of the free and the home of the brave !

Program from March 31, 1918

Stanley

THE DAY OF THE SOLDIER BOY

When it's morning on the border, and the sun
    is breaking through,
And the sands begin to glisten like the good
    old home town dew,
I look across the river, and it makes me kind
    of blue,
When it's morning on the border, Love, my
    thoughts go back to you.

When the sun is in the heavens and the air is
    mighty hot,
And it's hard to breathe and stifling, and my
    throat is dry as rot,
I've got to grin and bear it; I've got to see it
    through.
To make the burden lighter, Love, my
    thoughts go back to you.

When the sun has passed the border, and the
    after-glow is red,
And the silver moon is shining on the silent
    desert bed,
I'm feeling kind of lonely like, I know you're
    lonely too,
When the sun has passed the border, Love,
    my thoughts go back to you.

When the greaser stops his sniping and skulk-
    ing in the sand,
When the raider hies himself away beyond the
    Rio Grande.
And the "spick" doffs his sombrero to the old
    red, white and blue.
And it's calm along the border, Love, THEN
    I'LL COME BACK TO YOU.

HELL IN NEW MEXICO
BY THE AUTHOR OF "TEXAS A PARADISE"

The Devil in hell we're told was chained,
And a thousand years he there remained.
He neither complained nor did he groan,
But determined to start a hell of his own.

Where he could torment the souls of men
Without being chained in a prison pen,
So he asked the Lord if he had on hand
Anything left when he made this land.

The Lord said: "Yes, I had plenty on hand,
But I left it down on the Rio Grande;
The fact is 'old boy,' the stuff is so poor,
I don't think you can use it in hell any more."

But the devil went down to look at the truck,
And said if he took it as a gift he was stuck.
For after examining it carefully and well,
He concluded the place was too dry for a hell.

So in order to get it off His hand,
The Lord promised the Devil to water the land,
For he had some water, or rather some dregs,
A regular cathartic that smelled like bad eggs.

Hence the trade was closed, the deed was given,
And the Lord went back to His home in Heaven;
The Devil said to himself, "I have all that is needed
To make a good hell," and hence he succeeded.

He began by putting thorns all over the trees,
And mixed up the sand with millions of fleas;
He scattered tarantulas along the roads,
Put thorns on the cacti, and horns on the toads.

He lengthened the horns of the New Mexico steers,
And put an addition to the rabbits' ears;
He put a little devil in the broncho steed,
And poisoned the feet of the centipede.

The rattlesnake bites you, the scorpion stings,
The mosquito delights you with his buzzing wings;
The sand burrs prevail and so do the ants,
And those who sit down need half soles on their pants.

The Devil then said that throughout the land
He'd arranged to keep up the Devil's own brand,
And all should be Mavericks unless they bore
Marks of scratches, of bites and thorns by the score.

The heat in the summer is one hundred and ten,
Too hot for the Devil and too hot for men;
The wild boar roams through the black chaparral;
'Tis a hell of a place that he has for a hell.

Red Wing's National Guard Company L marches down Third Street past Sheldon Auditorium soon after the April 6, 1917, U.S. declaration of war against Germany.

Ticket stub found in Marland's uniform pocket years after his "missing in New York" caused a lot of concern [See page 89]

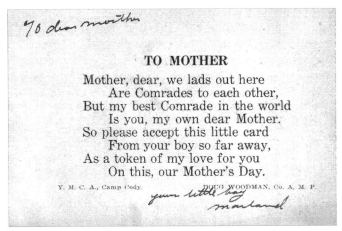

A Mother's Day card provided by the army signed "your little boy Marland"

Free Band Concert TONIGHT

Saturday, July 20th

at 7:30 o'clock, at the

Hospitality House

BY THE

125th Field Artillery Band

PROGRAMME

1. March—"Stars and Stripes Forever" .... Sousa
2. Overture—"Poet and Peasant" .... V. Suppe
3. Valse "Adele" .... Briquet
4. Selection—"Un Balle in Maschera" .... Verdi
5. Two Numbers From "Venetian Suite" ...... Nevin
   (a) Gondolieri
   (b) Canzone Amorosa
6. "Ballot Egyptien" .... Luigini
   (a) Alle non truppe
   (b) Allegrette
   (c) Andante Sostenute
   (d) Andante Expressive
7. Selection—"Traviata" .... Verdi
8. March—"Liberty Bell" .... Sousa
9. "STAR SPANGLED BANNER"

There will be a Short Dance after the Concert for the Enlisted Men

125th F. A. Band performance at Fort Sill

The 125th F. A. Band in France

Cannon Falls (Minnesota) Band. Marland is in front of bass drum.

Left: Stanley and his sisters Olga and Jewell

Above: Marland posed with his euphonium on the occasion of his 92nd birthday in 1991.

Left: Pictured in 1950 are, left to right, Marland, Olga, Jewell, Stanley.

Life After the War

Immediately after the war, Marland Williams worked as an auto mechanic in St. Paul. At church he was introduced to Elmie Strom, the girl mentioned in his letter of October 31, 1918. They were soon inseparable. At that time Elmie was attending Lutheran Bible Institute in St. Paul; her goal was to become a missionary. She encouraged Marland to become a physician so he could serve in the mission field with her. Despite not graduating from high school, his grades from Red Wing Seminary were good enough for admission to the University of Minnesota. The sweethearts were married in 1923. By the time Marland graduated from the U of M Medical School in 1930, they had two children, so they changed course and Marland took over a general medicine practice in Cannon Falls, Minnesota.

Elmie died in 1934, leaving Marland with three young children: Gerald, nearly seven years old, Keith, five, and eight-month-old Marilyn. Two years later Marland married Viola Grisim, who was known for her exquisite singing voice. She gave him another son, Roger. Viola died in 1949 when Roger was eleven. In 1953 Doc Williams married a third time. Phyllis (nee Wallace) Rogers brought Richard and Greg, her sons from a previous marriage, to the family. She worked alongside Marland as a nurse anesthetist.

Marland practiced medicine in Cannon Falls for forty years. He was responsible for a new medical arts building, chaired the Blood Bank of Southeastern Minnesota, and was twice named Outstanding General Practitioner of Goodhue County. He served as Draft Examiner for the district, was board chair of St. Ansgar's Lutheran Church for 13 years, and was a member of the Coast Guard Auxiliary.

On Sunday, April 20, 1969, Cannon Falls celebrated Marland's long and dedicated service to the community with a huge public event called Doc Williams Day. The high school gymnasium was packed with people eager to share their Doc Williams stories. By this time he had delivered more than 2,000 children, who proudly wore buttons for the occasion declaring, "I am a Williams Baby"—including my siblings and me.

Despite his demanding medical practice, Marland still found time to play his double-bell euphonium with the Cannon Falls Band—sometimes as a soloist—in the WPA band shell he helped to get built.

In 1975 Marland and Phyllis retired to Eustis, Florida. He died there on August 22, 1994, at the age of 95 years. She died in 2002. Marland and Phyllis are buried in Cannon Falls Cemetery.

Upon returning from the war, Stanley Williams got a job at the 1st National Bank in St. Paul. There he rose through the ranks from teller to become the bank auditor. He was an active member of the American Legion, and served as Chef de Gare (literally, station master) of the St. Paul Voiture (literally, a conveyance for travel; a local unit of the Forty-and-Eight).[78] Influenced by his family's love of music, Stanley enjoyed playing saxophone in local dance bands.

Stanley and his sisters never married and lived with their parents in a two-story farmhouse surrounded by open fields at 1530 Burns Avenue in St. Paul. It was said Stanley suffered some lung damage from exposure to gas during the war, and as a result, strenuous work was difficult for him. Soon after their father died in 1936, it was decided to sell the family home with Alvin's extensive and bountiful garden. The three siblings and their mother moved to a charming stucco home at 855 Sherwood Avenue. Hulda passed away in 1945.

Olga, Jewell, and Stanley—"O.J.S." as they were affectionately known—were outstanding hosts for large festive family gatherings at their home. Compared to his energetic sisters, Stan was a quiet fellow, quick to help when asked, but otherwise content to sit in his comfortable chair. He died at the age of 86 on November 10, 1982.

After Stan's passing, Olga and Jewell moved into a modern townhouse. Both women had enjoyed professional careers that afforded them frequent world adventures. They loved showing their souvenir hats and home movies of their trips to the extended family. Olga passed away on October 23, 1989. Jewell died March 15, 2002.

Alvin, Hulda, and their four remarkable children are deeply missed by those who knew them, for they truly lived "with love to all."

—E. W. G.

78. The Forty & Eight was organized in 1920 as an elite society for leaders of the American Legion. The name comes from the French boxcar that was familiar to WWI troops. On each car's side was painted its cargo capacity "40/8," meaning it could carry forty men and eight horses. A French railroad theme was used for officers' titles and organizational functions.

Sources

Marland R. Williams's interesting, conversational letters and the wide-ranging scope of his photograph collection can stand alone as a valid historical overview of the 125th Field Artillery story from its Minnesota National Guard days to federalization and incorporation into the U.S. Army. His work makes up the first and largest part of *With love to all.* Williams described almost every aspect of the Minnesota 125th Field Artillery's nearly year-long training experience at Camp Cody, New Mexico. The first portion of this book is, for the most part, based on his letters.

A helpful publication with supporting contextual information to Marland's story of life at Camp Cody is *Reveille*, a newsletter published by the 136th Infantry and issued to soldiers at Camp Cody. It lacks the photography of the Williams archive, but also tells of those who trained for war at the New Mexico base. *Reveille* is found in the collections of the Minnesota Historical Society. The Red Wing National Guard company was among units merged into 125th Field Artillery. Harvey Johnson's history of one element of the 125th—Lt. Harvey Johnson, "Company L" in *Goodhue County in the World War* (Red Wing: Red Wing Printing Co., 1919) 183–185—gives information about the artillery outfit's training and follows its movements across the U.S. and while in France.

L. Stanley Williams provided an interesting series of letters regarding his experiences with the 151st Field Artillery, 42nd Rainbow Division, in the second section of *With love to all.* Since, by necessity, his letters underwent both self-censorship and official review, his notes home—although illuminating about his life in combat—were fairly general. Books written in the immediate aftermath of the war were most helpful in understanding the many trials Stanley and his Rainbow Division comrades experienced but could not write about. Louis L. Collins, author of *History of the 151st Field Artillery* (St. Paul: War Records Commissions, 1924), wrote with firsthand knowledge, having been a member of this prominent Minnesota unit. Collins, who had been a former newspaper reporter and was Minnesota's lieutenant governor at the time he wrote his 151st F. A. history, provides an excellent starting point. The Collins book is also included in Franklin Holbrook and Livia Appel's *Minnesota in the War with Germany*, Vol. 1, "History of the 151st Field Artillery," (St. Paul: Minnesota War Records Commission, 1928). Holbrook also wrote *St. Paul and Ramsey County in the War of 1917–18* (St. Paul: Ramsey County War Records Commission, 1929). George Leach, the only commander to lead the 151st F. A., kept a diary of events— George Leach, *War Diary* (Minneapolis: Pioneer Printers, 1923 n.p.)—that reports operational and combat details, along with copies of field orders.

The Minnesota Historical Society has useful, accessible information regarding the state's First World War years. Among the sources employed for this study were Minnesota War Records Commission, *Bulletins, Circulars and Newsletters, 1918–1925 and Collected Materials, 1900–1936.* The papers of Rollo Lester Mudge and William K. Fraser, both members of the 151st Field Artillery provide a variety of materials—correspondence, photos, papers, pay books—and Fraser's wartime diary.

Michael Kromeke has established a website dedicated to preserving the story of Camp Cody during World War I. It is easy to navigate and rich with images and descriptions. http://demingnewmexico.genealogyvillage.com/Camp Cody

Image Credits

As noted earlier in the Transcribing the Letters section of this book, nearly all images included here are from the collections of Marland and Stanley Williams. The photo on page 96 comes from the Rollo L. Mudge Papers; the program on page 98 is found in the William K. Fraser Papers. Photographs on page 109, 112, and 119 are from Collins, *History of the 151st Field Artillery.* The photograph of the Red Wing Seminary Band is held by St. Olaf College Archives, Northfield, Minnesota. Photographs appearing on the back cover and the page adjacent to "Artifacts of War" are by Betsy Wall, Rochester, Minnesota.

Index

MW = Marland Williams
SW = Stanley Williams

–A–

Allied Nations, 7; casualties, 121
Alvin Williams General Merchandise (store), 3–4, *4*
Alvin Williams Grocery Store, 4, 36
American Legion, 145–46, 146n, Forty & Eight, 146, 146n
American woman (by naturalization) An, 15
Anderson, Ellen "Elen" Peterson (aunt), 42, 68n
Anderson, Ludwig, 19n
Anderson, Roy, discharge, 32; illness of, 17, 24, 28, 28n
Andrew, Louy, 45
Andrews, Gust, 35
Army of Occupation, 122
Asp, C., 27

–B–

Bach, Frank, 19n
Baker, Secretary of War Newton Diehl, 37, 37n
Battery B (Batt, B/Battery "B,"/Bat. B), 46, 50; corral,
Battery C (Battery "C,"/Bat. "C"), 98n60, 102n, 107, 108
Bay City (Wisconsin), 28n, 45
Benson, Irvine, 19n
Blocksane, Gen. (Blocksom, Gen. Augustus P.), 13, 13n5
Brown, John C., 19n
Burnquist/Burndquist, Gov. (Burnquist, Gov. Joseph A. A.), 24, 24n15, 25

–C–

Camp Cody (NM), 7, *8*, 12n, 15, *20*, 31, *34*, *35*, *36*, 40, 41, 42, *46*, 50n, 55n, 60n, 65, *65*, 67, 108n; Camp Cody Song, *21*; health of soldiers, 14, 16, 16n, 20n11, 20–22, 26–27, 28, 32, 50, 50n; impression of, 14; military funerals, 26n, *27*, 33; movie, 42; remount station, 34n; saxophone group, *51*; show movies of in St. Paul, 40, 42
Camp Deming (NM), *12*, 12n
Camp Dodge (IA), 89
Camp Grant (IL), 11
Camp Merritt (NJ), 81n, 89
Camp Mills (NY), 81, 81n, 84n, 95, 95n, 97, 99
Camp Upton (NJ), 80n44, 80–81, *81*, 81n, *82*, 83, 84, 84n; remount station, 81, *81*

Campbell, Louie, 107
Cannon Falls Band, 58, *144*, 145; WPA band shell, 145
Caldwell, Lt., 115
Central Powers, 7, 121
Chalons (France), 116
Champagne (France), 108, 109, province, 128
Champagne-Marne, 110, 116; offensive, *110*, 111
Chateau-Thierry (France), 93, 112, 128, *128*
Coblenz. *See* Koblenz.
Company L, 19, 19n, 20n10, 22, 24, 28n, 46, 48, 52n, 68, *142*
Cox, Capt. Theodore S. (censor), 84, 86, 87
Creskill (NJ), 89
Croix de Guerre, 111n, 124, 124n74, 124n75
Cussac (France), 83

–D–

Daillecourt (France), location, 113, *128*
Danielson, Pvt. Charles, 124n74; *Croix de Guerre*, 124
Deming (NM), 13, 26, 30, 31, 42, *43*, 65
Duluth (MN), 4, *5*, 19, 56; MW goes to, 4; last time in house before leaving for training, 22; National Guard Headquarters Company, 11, 19
Duluth Company A, 7

–E–

8th Division, off to France, 76
83rd Infantry Brigade, 115
84th Infantry Brigade, 115
Eldrdge, Miss, 119
Emily, Aunt (Emelie/Emelia), 43, 53, 109
Europe, letters from Marland and Stanley, 1, 88
Erickson, Pete, 32n; burial, 32n; death, 32–33; illness of, 17, 20, 23–24, 26, 27, 29, 31, 31n, 32; insurance, 37, 48

–F–

Fauts (Fouts), Ray, 46n, 46–47, 49
1st Field Artillery, 4, 7; renamed, 94n
4th Division, 113
5th Army, 119
42nd "Rainbow" Division, *94*, 94n, 108, 111, 112, 113, 115, 116, 118, 121, *140–1*; attached to 6th French Army, 112; casualties, 113, 117, 119; field dressing station, *111*; marching into Germany, 93
44th Street Theater (NY), 89, *143*

First Lutheran Church (St. Paul), 29, 86n
Flynn, Albert, 19n, 67–68
Fort Sill (OK), 11, 41, 65, *65*, 118, 143; balloon
    accident, 75, *75*, 75n; MW comparison to Camp
    Cody, 65, 67, 77; left Fort Sill, 83; plane landing,
    66; School of Fire for Field Artillery, 65n
Fort Snelling (MN), signs at, 45
France, *7*, *11*, 15, *18*, 34, 37, 39, 42, *60*, 66, *71*, 76,
    76, 81, 81n, *83*, 85, 85n50, 94n, 96n, *117*, 127,
    127; casualties, 121; life in, 108; map of, *65*; U.S.
    soldiers serving in, 51, 89, 93, 97, 102, 108n
Fredolf/Fridolph, 106, 108
French Army Corps, 116; treatment of Germans
    at end of war, 123
Ft. Cuming (NM) (Fort Cummings), 55; location
    of, 55n

–G–
Gerdeen, Christen. *See* Girdeen, Christine.
Germany, casualties, 121; German people, 123; life
    in, 123n; map of, *65*
Girdeen, Christine (Christin), death, 32; care of
    Pete Erickson, 23–24, 29, 31–32; marriage to
    Daniel M. Olander, 32; Pete's insurance, 37, 48;
    residence, 32
Gomoll, Elizabeth Williams (granddaughter of
    MW), 1, 5, 61n, 146
Gouraud, Gen., 116
Goutfred, (Gotfried), Loyd T., 29
Grant, Rev., 29, 35, 103
Great War, 7; use of *Star Spangled Banner* during, 30
Grisim, Viola, marriage to MW, 145
Gustafson, Albin O., 18, 19n, 22, 28n, 29, 29n 19,
    54, 64, 67

–H–
Hager City (Wisconsin), 18, 19
Heimersheim (Germany), location, 121, 128, *128*
Hinckley (MN), 68, 68n, 71
Hoboken (NJ), port of embarkation, *80*, 89
Hofflander, 1ˢᵗ Lt. H. F. (censor), 87
Holter (soldier), 27
Hullander, Arthur, 19n, 28n; birth, 20n10; illness
    of, 20, 23, 26, 27, 28, 40
Hullander, Fred (Carl Frederick), 23, 24n13, 31
Hullander, Gottfred (Gotfred), 19n, 68
Hulmquist, William, 76, 87

–I–
Irvine, Chester W., 19n, 29, 48

–J–
Jacobson, 2ⁿᵈ Lt. D. (censor), 88
Jerdeen, Miss. *See* Girdeen, Christine.
John, Uncle, 109
Johnson, Frederick L., 19n

–K–
Kask, Clarence, 66n, 71; leave for funeral, 66
Kish, Clifford E., 19n
Knutsen, Sen. (Rep. Harold Knutson), 15, 15n
Koblenz (Germany), 123, 127, *128*
Korseland (Korslund, Milo Franklin), death, 76–77

–L–
Larson, Hulda. *See* Williams, Hulda.
Lawton (OK), 69n39, 77; and wife, 71; leave for
    funeral, 66; relation to MW and SW, 66n
Leach, Col. George A., 111; honors, 111n
Long Island (NY), 11, 41, 84n
Lorraine (France), 102, 116; map of, 128, *128*

–M–
Mackuster, John, 53
McAdoo, William, development of Liberty Bonds,
    29n20
McCoy, 2ⁿᵈ Lt. Everett F. (censor), 102, 109,
    110, 114
McKeen, Roy E., 19n
Medicine Creek (in OK), 69n
Medicine Park (OK), 69, 69n
Medoc (France), 89
Menoher, Gen. Charles, laudatory statement SW
    and fellow soldiers, 116–7
Meurcy-Ferme (France), 116
Meuse-Argonne (France), offensive, 93, 93n54,
    118, 119
Mexican Revolution, 52n
Minnesota National Guard, 4, 7, 60n, *137*
Minnesota State Fair, 76, 78
Mississippi River, 3, 14n, 18

–N–
Nadeau, Eugene, 19n
National Personnel Records Center, 5
Neusen, Lt. G. C. (censor), 100, 101
New Mexico, 52n; map of, *65*
New York City, 89, 114

–O–
125ᵗʰ Field Artillery (125ᵗʰ F.A.), *8*, *41*, *48*, 72, 89,
    108, 118; band, *15*, *27*, 30, *37*, 40, 45, *49*, *51*, *57*,
    85, 108n; head to Fort Sill, 11, 41; sign at Fort
    Snelling, 45; training, 41, *54*; trip to Europe, 11;
    troop trains, *63*, *64*
151ˢᵗ Field Artillery (151ˢᵗ F.A.), 7, 37, 93, 94n, 113,
    118, 119, 121, 124n74, 128n; arrival in France,
    97n, 102, 126; battlefield duties and postings,
    98, 102, 104, 106, 108, 109, 111, 112, 113, 117,
    119; casualties, 98, 109, 112, 117, 124n74, 127;
    commander Stanley, 119; drive to Montfaucon,
    118; giving passes, 127; music program, *100*;
    soldiers received *Croix de Guerre*, 124n74

treatment of German at end of war, 123; weapons, 98, *98*, 98n60, 106n68, 111, 113

Olson, Arthur M., 19n, 48

Oklahoma, map of, *65*

Ourcq River (France), 112, 113, 116

–P–

Paris, 113, 114, 128; map of, *128*, passes to, 127

Pershing, Gen. John J., 52n

Petersen, Theodor, *Croix de Guerre*, 124n74; U.S. Distinguished Service Cross, 124n74

Peterson, Alvin. *See* Williams, Alvin.

Peterson, Arvid. *See* Williams, Arvid.

Peterson, Ed (Edd) (uncle), 35, 35n, 53, 112

Peterson, Lillian, 14

Peterson, Oscar Wilhelm. *See* Williams, Oscar.

Peterson, Sidney, 19, 34, 35, 43, 53, 66, 88, 109, 118

Peterson, Theodore, 19n, 118

Pierce County (Wisconsin), 3, 19, 19n, 35n

President Lincoln, 96n

–R–

Rainbow Division. *See* 42nd "Rainbow" Division.

Randall, B. M. (censor), 120

Red Cross, 9, 14, 20, 53, *64*, 70, 79

Red Wing (MN), 3, *5*, 18, 24, 32, *53*, 93; house in, 53n32

Red Wing Seminary, 3, 13n4, 19, 93, 137, 145; band, *137*

Red Wing-Trenton Connection, 18–19, 19n

Rhine River, 121, 123, 124

Roach, Francis F., 19n

Rogers, Greg (stepson), 145

Rogers, Phyllis (Wallace), career, 145; death, 145; marriage to MW, 145

Rogers, Richard (MW's stepson) 145

Russia, 72

2nd Battalion, Headquarters Company, 93

6th French Army, 112

72nd Division, 118

–S–

Saint-Nazaire (France), 128, *128*

Sedan (France), 119, *128*

Scott, 1st Lt. H. H. (censor), 122, 124

Serbia. *See* Siberia.

Services of Supply (S.O.S.), 113, 120, 122, 128n

Sharp (Sharpe), Harold, 19n, 28, 28n, 67

Siberia, 76; trip to, 72

Smidth Family, 14

Smidt, Art, (Smith, Arthur E.), 16, *16*, 19n, 28n, 29, 40, 45, 48, 54, 68, 74

Sorenson (visitor), 33

SS Saxon, 82n, 83

SS Tuscania, 27n

St. Louis (MO), 5

St. Mihiel (France), 93, 93n54, 115, 128, *128. Also* Saint-Mihiel.

St. Paul (MN), *5*, 13n6, *66*, *71*, 85, 95, 96, 115; family moves to, 4; letters regarding Fort Snelling sign, 45; live in home and find jobs, 71; MW's comparison to New York, 81; see Clarence Kast in, 66; SW and sisters live in, 145; SW thinking about going home, 123

Strom, Elmie, 86, 145; death, 145; marriage to MW, 86n, 145; study to be missionary, 145

Strom, John, 86n

Strom, Matilda, 86n

Strothman, Lyle V., 19n

Summerall, Gen. Charles, 119

Sundell, Carl E., 19n

Svea (Wisconsin) (community), 3, 18, 19, 43, 62, 102

Svea boys, 16, 28n, 29, 40, 48, 54, 67, 87

Svea Lutheran Church, 3, *5*, 19, 20n10, 29n19

Swanson, Ted, 106

–T–

32nd Division, 118

34th "Sandstorm" Infantry Division, 7, 11, *20*, *39*, 76; conversion to artillery, 17; nickname, 11; training, 41, 60n; training at Camp Cody, 11, 11n2, 19

Taggart, Lloyd J., 19n

Third Minnesota Infantry, 3, 4, 11, 128n

Town of Trenton (Wisconsin) (Trenton Township), 3, 18, 35n

Trenton (Wisconsin) (village), 23, 31, 32, 96

–U–

U.S. Army, 5, 7, 60n; casualties, 121; Minnesota National Guard nationalized, 7, 60; of Occupation, 121, 122, 123, 128; personnel records destroyed, 5

Ulvin, Orion, 13

–V–

Vesle River (France), 113

Violet (dog), *45*

–W–

Wiberg, Lesile (Leslie), 18, 35

Wiberg, Pearly, 56, 76

Williams, Alvin (Pa/Papa/Daddy), *4*, *5*, 31, 33, 37, 38, 53; as storekeeper, 4, 18, 71, 105; cactus, 67; church membership, 29, 38; dislike of cigars, 100; immigration to America, 3; importance of music to family, 3, 35; interest in flowers/gardens, 45, 61, 112; joking about clothing kids, 43; live in Town of Trenton, 18; marriage, 3; money for horn, 61–62, 63, 66–67; move to St.

Paul, 13n6, 97, 146; moving to new home, 35, 36; MW wants photo of, 77; name change, 3; not in photos, 15, 45; peripatetic lifestyle, 3, 35, 38, 53, 53n32, 70–71, 117; permission to use bonds, 77; pride in SW, 56; snacking, 23; trips to train station for MW, 89

Williams, Arvid, name change, 3

Williams, Gerald (MW's son), 83, 145

Williams, Hulda Larson (Mamma/Mother), *4, 5,* 13, 100, 100n; assist in store, 4; church membership, 29; immigration to America, 3; letters to SW in Swedish, 100, 100n; marriage, 3; move to St. Paul, 70–71, 146; MW needs towels, 36; MW wants photo of, 36, 45, 77; new store, 18; not in photos, 15; work on pillow, 13

Williams, Jewell Hazel Mildred (sister), *4, 5,* 15, 43, *144;* assist in store, 4, 18; birth 3; death, 146; importance of music to family, 3, 35, 45, 49, 62, 78; knitting, 33; MW wants photo of, 36; photo of, 45, 88; residence in St. Paul, 146; school, 27

Williams, Keith (MW's son), 145

Williams, (Lawrence) Stanley (Standley/Standly/Standely), *2, 4,* 47, 50–51, 57, 66, 71, 77, *92, 102, 141, 144;* accommodations, 123; allotment, 95, 97, 99, 101–2, 110, 114, 115, 118, 119, 125–26; and armistice, 122, 125; battles, 93; birth 3; camp life, 101, 103, 104–5, 110, 117–8, 120, 122, 127; celebrating Christmas, 101, 124; Christmas wishes, 119, 119n, 120; church membership, 103; community involvement, 145–6; condition updates, *104, 126;* death, 146; dental work, 127; discharge, *130;* education, 3, 13n4, 19; employment at 1st National Bank, 145; employment at Merchants Bank, 4, 93, 95, 96; discussion of MW's posting, 94; enlistment, 4, 93, *129;* exposure to poison gas, 102, 106, 107n, 146; going home, 122, 125, 128n; going overseas to France, 96; has a girl, 29, 31; Headquarters Company 126, *140–1;* in France, 51, 93, 97, 108; in Germany, 122–4; insurance policy, 97, 99; invited to dinner, 95; joking with MW, 97; length of time in France, 116; letters, 1, 7, *8,* 9, 38, 53, 63, 74, 94–128; letters from MW, 105, 107, 122, 125; march to Germany, 93, 122, 125; military duties, 94, 99; music, 3, 146; MW gets letter from, 50–51; not getting letters from MW, 101, 108, 114, 115, 119, 120, 123, 125; packages received, 99–100, 100–1, 103, 124–5; package request, 109; pass to Paris, 113, 114, 115, 127; photography, 1, 102, 107; possibility of MW's coming over, 99, 103, 106, 110, 112, 114; preparation to go overseas, 94; promotions, 93, 102, 103, 120; regiment location, 102; residence in St. Paul, 146; response to MW's not getting his letters, 96; treatment of Germans "Boche, "Hun," 106, 106n67, 107, 114, 118;

use of shorthand, 110; wages, 95, 99, 105; war souvenirs, 114, 118–9, 120, 125; with saxophone, *137;* with Headquarters Company, 126; WWI service, 1, 18

Williams, Marilyn (MW's daughter), 145

Williams, Marland Reinhold "Kid," *2, 4, 10, 50,* 118, *144;* armistice signed, 88, 88n; arrival in France, 83, *84,* 88n; assignment to Third Minnesota Infantry Band, 3, 11; birth, 3; border protection, 51–52, 52n; camp life (Camp Cody), 1, 13, 15–16, 17–18, 19–20, *22,* 22n, 22–23, *23,* 24, *25,* 25–26, 27, 28, 33–35, *35,* 36, 37, *38,* 38–41, 42–43, 44, 45–46, *46, 47,* 52, 53, 55, *55,* 56, 57, *60,* 60–61, 67; camp life (Fort Sill) 65–66, 67, *68,* 69, *69,* 72, 74, 75, 77; Cannon Falls celebrates Doc Williams Day, 145; community involvement, 145; concerts/funerals/programs, 13, 17–18, 23, 25, 26, 26n, 27, 28, 30, *30,* 32, 34, 36, 37, *38,* 38–39, 40, 41, 42, 44–45, 48, 49, 51, *51,* 53, 56, 57, *57,* 60, 62, 63, 66, 67, 68, 69, 70, 72, 74, 75, 76, 77, 79, 83, 85, 87, 88; death, 145; dental work, 13, 47, 72; discharge, 11, *91;* double-bell euphonium ("horn"), 1, 57, 58, *58, 59,* 60, 61n, 61–62, 63, 68, 72, 89, *144,* 145; education, 3, 4, 13n4, 19; employed as auto mechanic, 145; enlistment, *6, 90;* exhibition of uniform and contents, 89; family, 145; first marriage, 86n, 145; gas drills, 42, *42,* 44, 44n; health of soldiers on boat, 83; illness, 89, 125, 127; immunization, 12; importance of music to family, 3, 35; insurance policy, 24, 24n14, 37; laundry, 1, 48, 52, 68, *68,* 74; leave for home, 89; letters, 1, 7, *8,* 9, 12–88; Liberty Bonds, 29, 29n20, 35, 47, 62, 71, 77; meatless and wheatless days, 40, 40n, medical career, 145; "missing," 5, 12, 89, *89,* 125; music, 3, 11, 14, 15, 105, 127; overseas orders, 64; packages received, 13–14, 17, 25, 27, 39, 45, 55, 69, 72, *87;* photography, 1, 11, 72; practice medicine in Cannon Falls, 145; preparation to go overseas, 11, 50, 53, 63, 69, 70, 72, 75–76, 77, 78, 79, 80, 82, 82n; privations noted in France, 86; retirement, 145; second marriage, 145; souvenirs, 5, 43, 78, 89, 112–3, *143;* state pride, 42; study medicine at University of Minnesota Medical School, 145; third marriage, 145; travel to Elpaso (El Paso) TX, 64; trip to go overseas, 78–79, *79,* 83; uncertainty about Stanley, 17, 18, 19, 22, 23, 24, 25–26, 27, 34, 35, 40, 42, 46, 48, 49, 50, 56, 61, 67, 68, 74, 76, 78, 84, 86, 87, 88; wages, 15–16, 29, 35, 47; weapons used, 17, 43, *43,* 52; with cornet, *137;* WWI service, 1

Williams, Olga Serafia Constantine (sister), *4, 5,* 15, 31, 32, 34, 39, 54, 60, 88, *144;* assist in store, 4; birth 3; confirmation, 53, 53n31, 56; death, 146; illness, 23; importance of music to family, 3, 13,

35, 45, 49, 77–78; knitting, 33; money matters, 47, 66–67, 101–2; MW teasing about weight, 5, 36, 40, 49, 56, 72; new clothes, 43; residence in St. Paul, 146; school, 27; typewriting, 87; use of camera, 72, 74, 77; volunteering with Red Cross, 70; Williams, Oscar, name change, 3

Williams, Roger (MW's son), 145

Wilson, Woodrow (president), 40; and The Star Spangled Banner, 30; declaration of war, 7; re-election, 7

–Y–

YMCA (Y.M.C.A./Y/Y.M.CA), *8*, 9, 36, *36*, 40, 70, 75, 78, 115, 137; British YMCA, 115

Made in the USA
Middletown, DE
03 June 2017